SNAIL
COLORING BOOK FOR KIDS

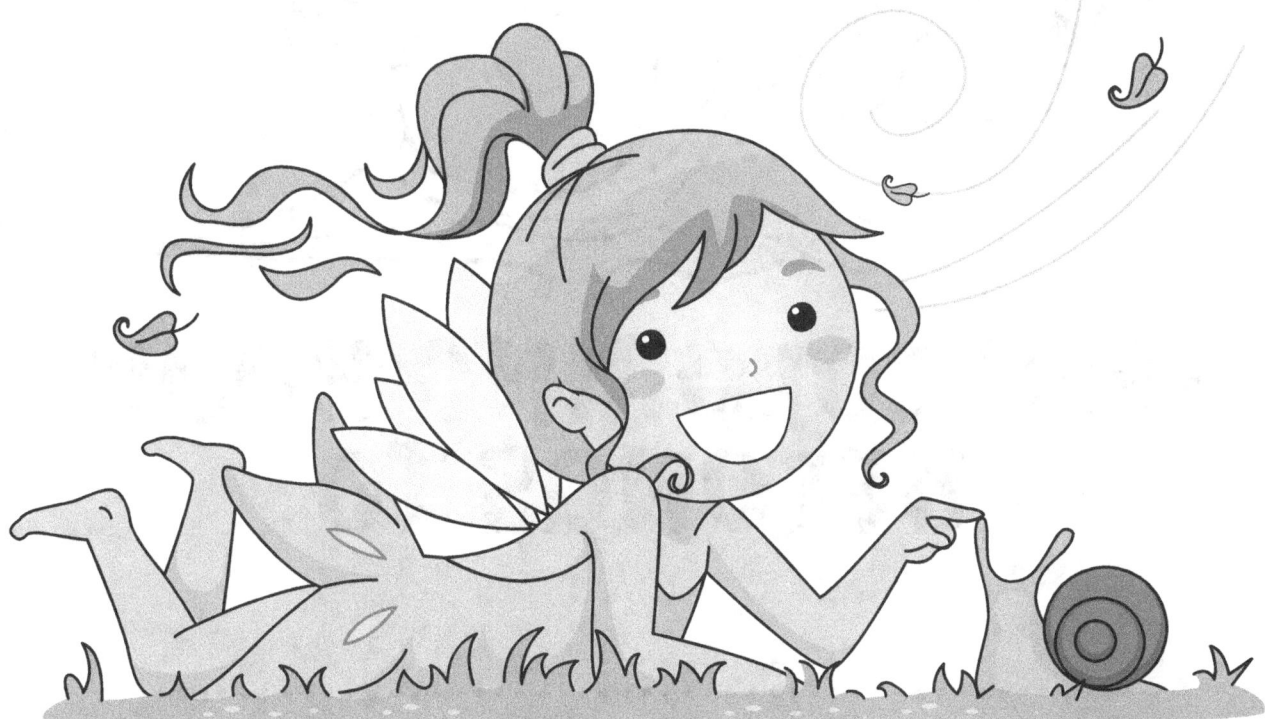

AGES 6-10

35 COLORING WORLD

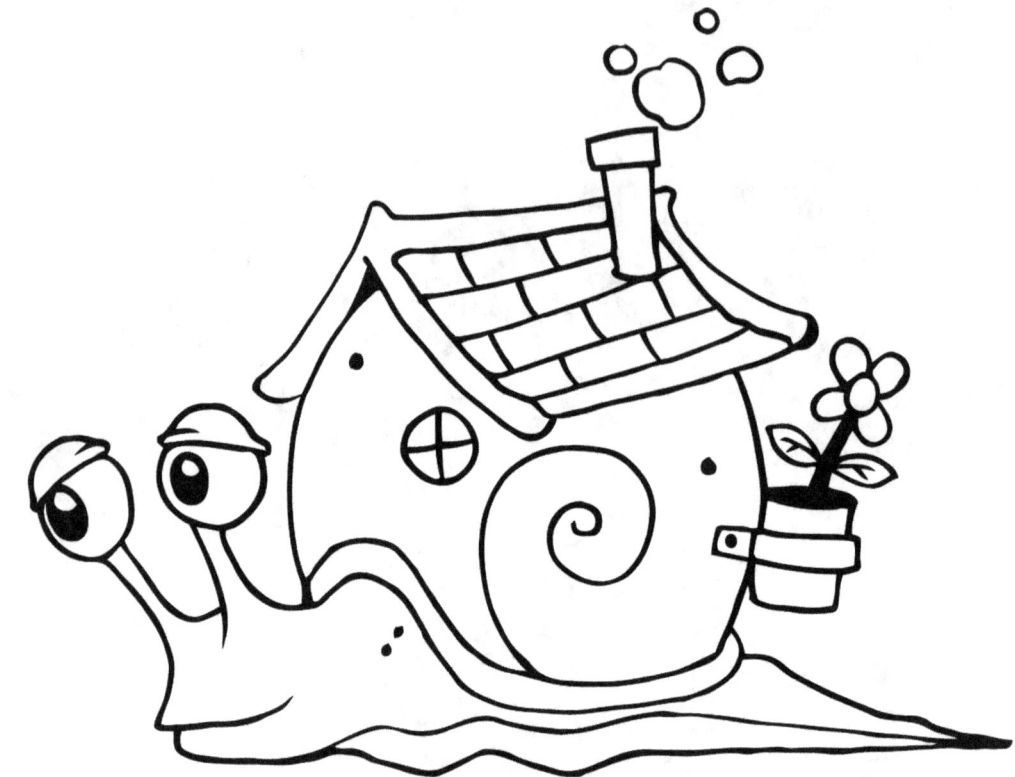

THIS COLORING BOOK BELONGS TO

....

....

....

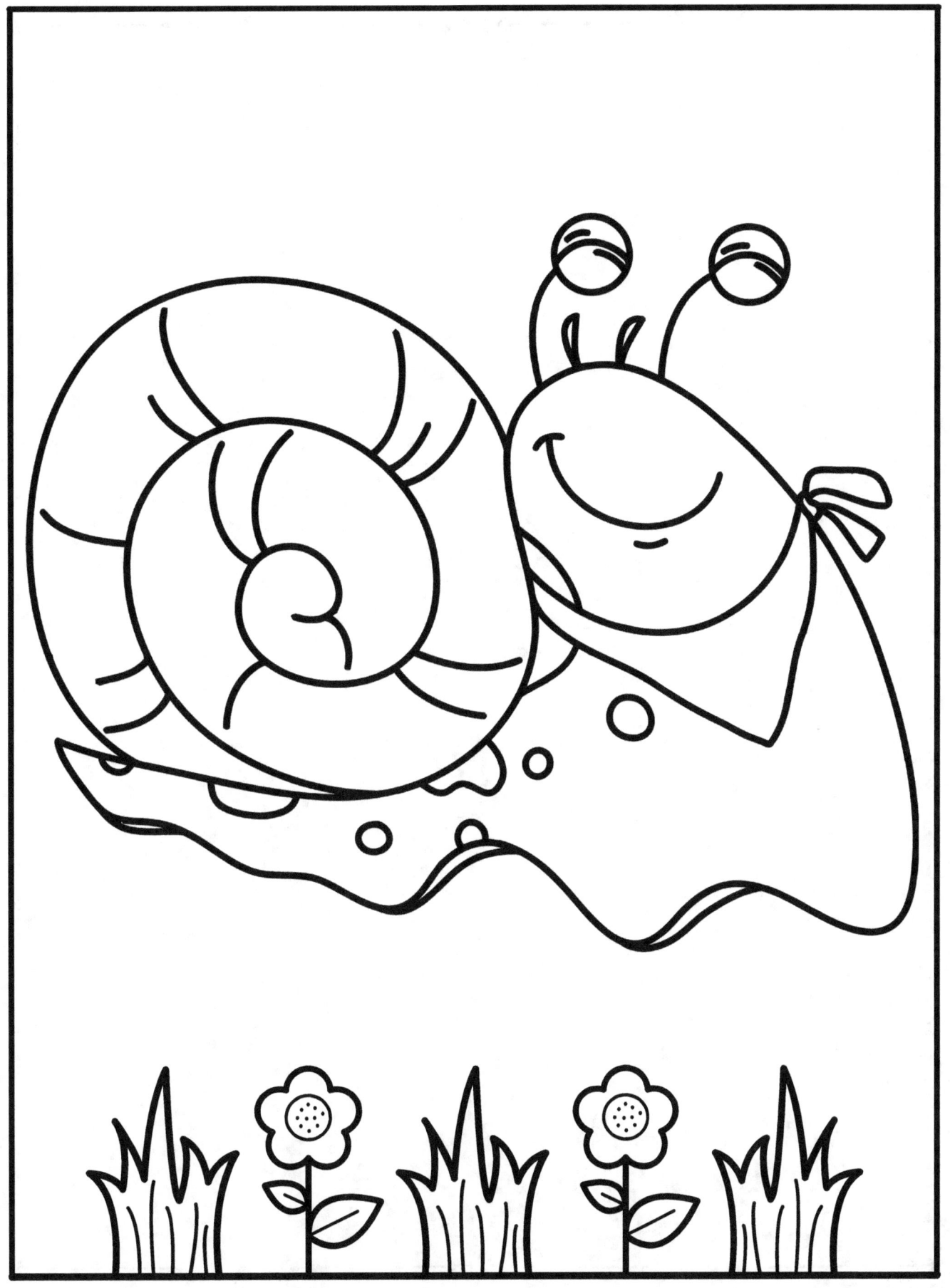

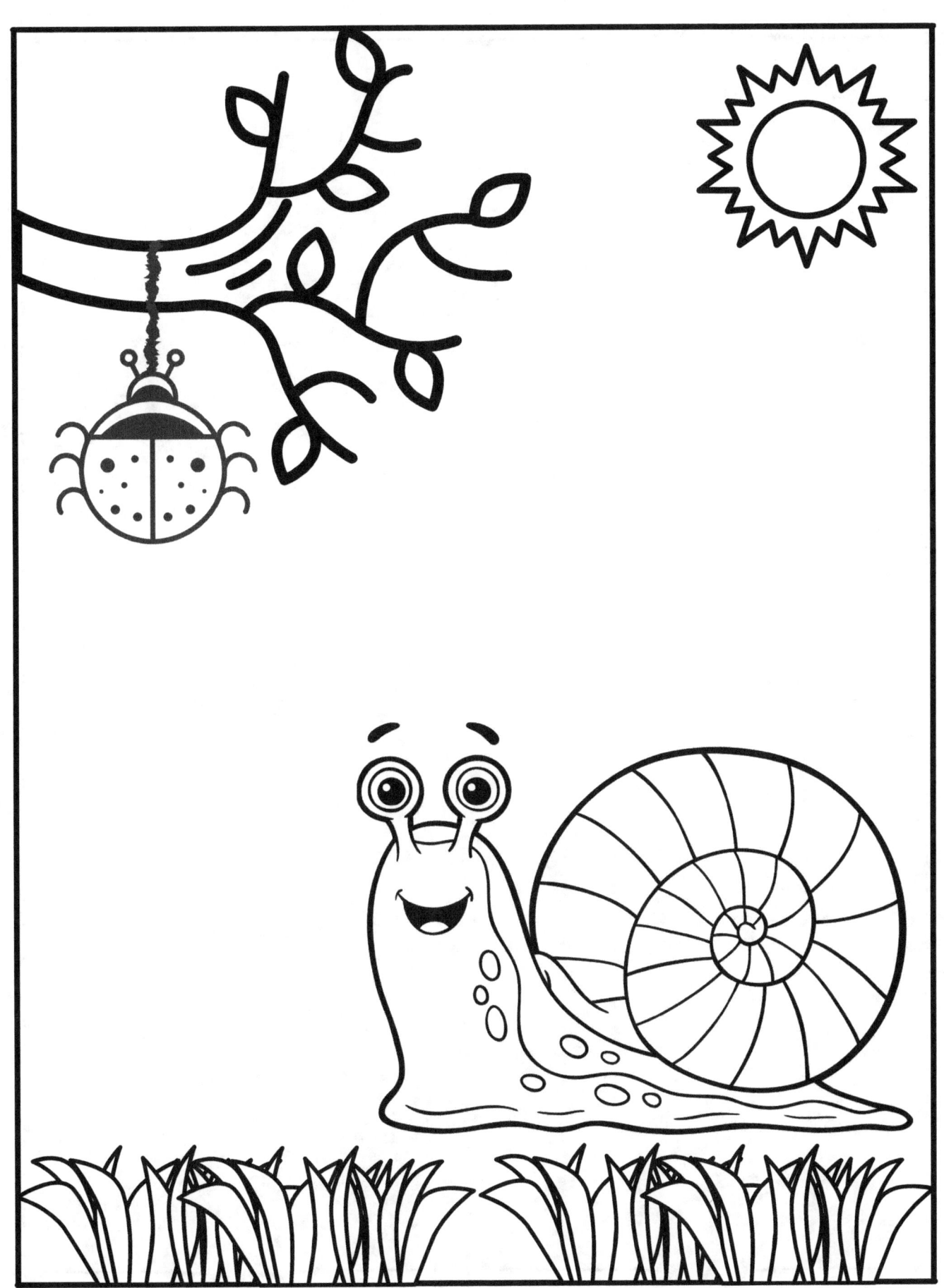

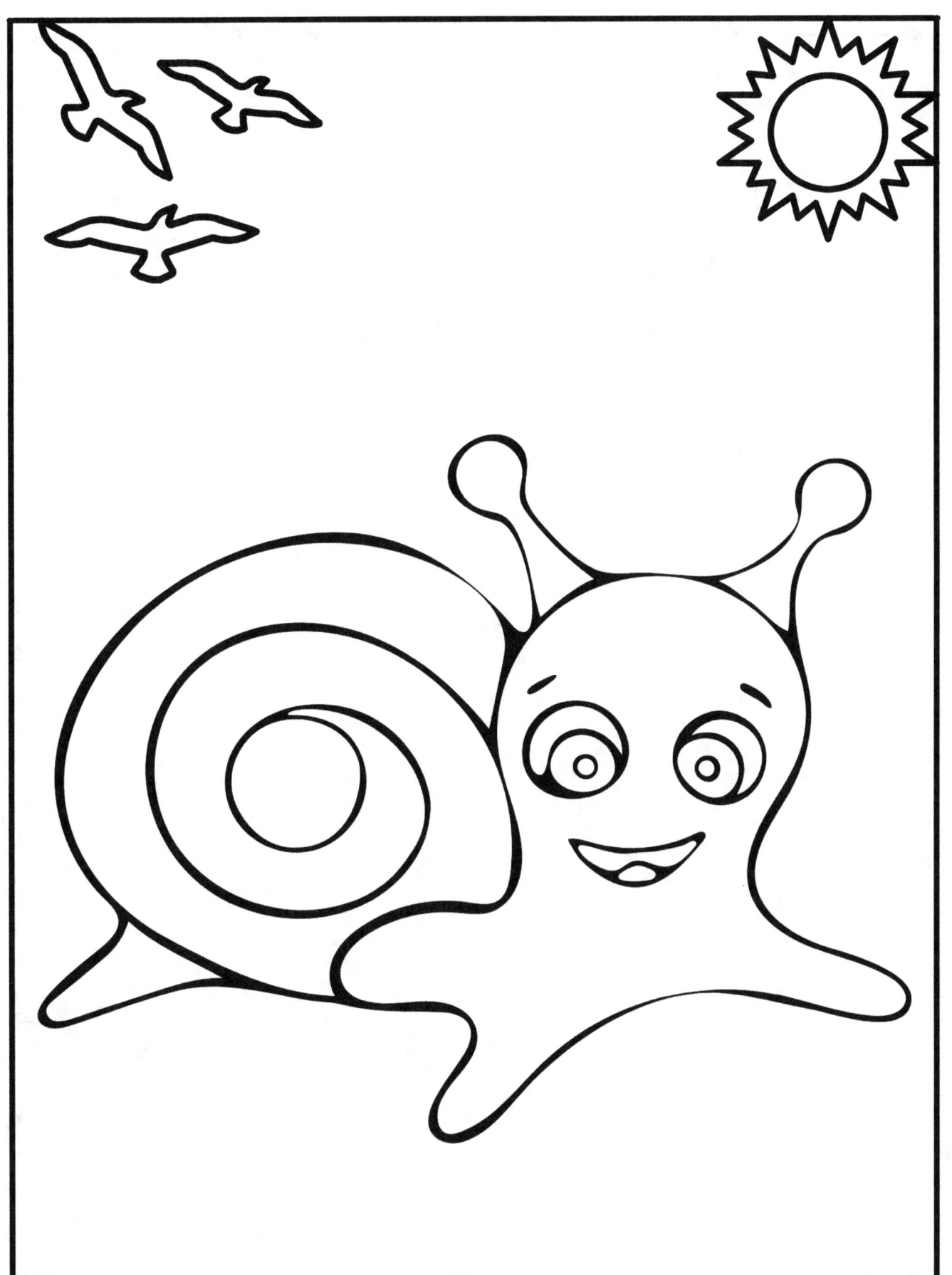

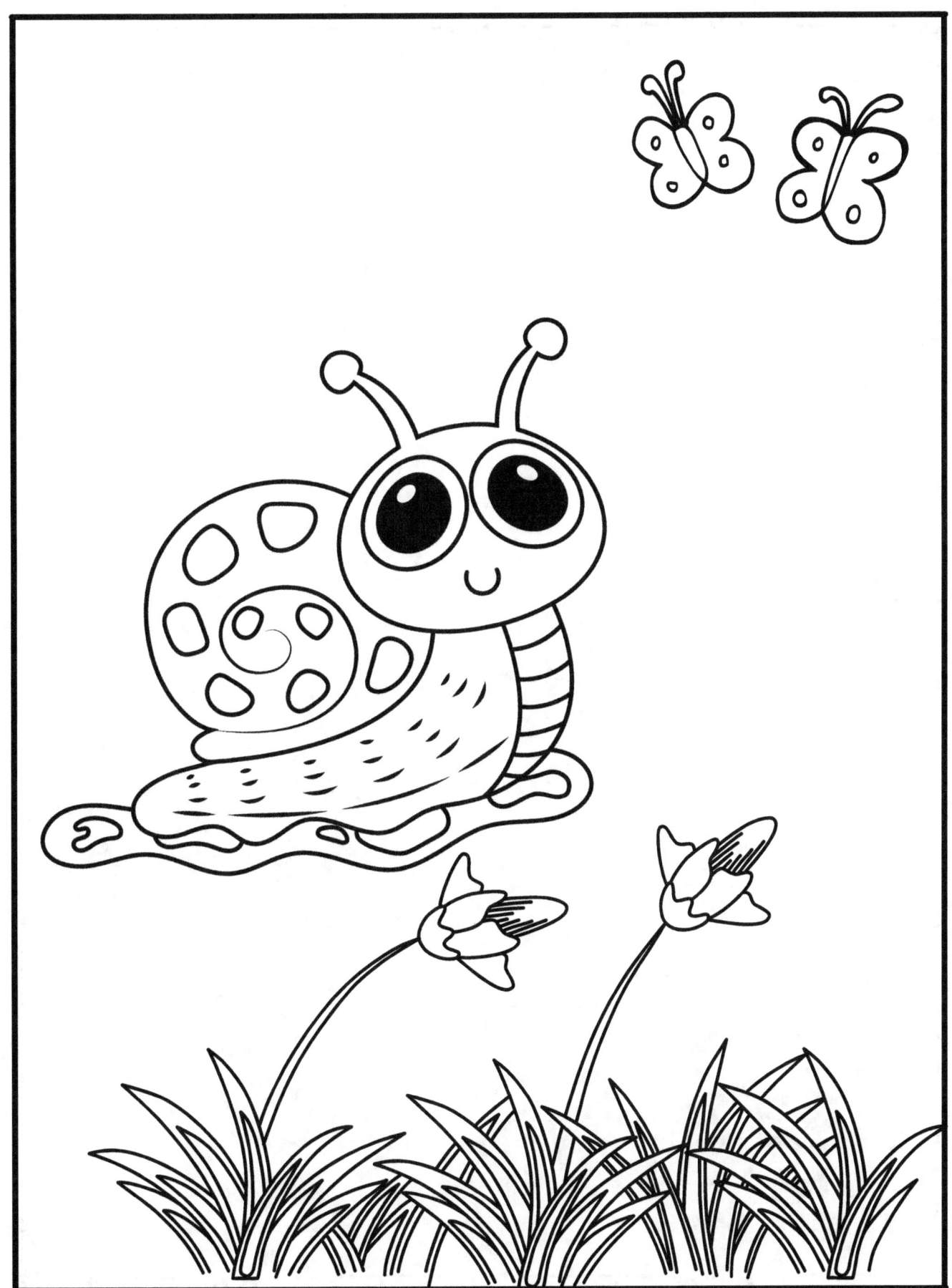

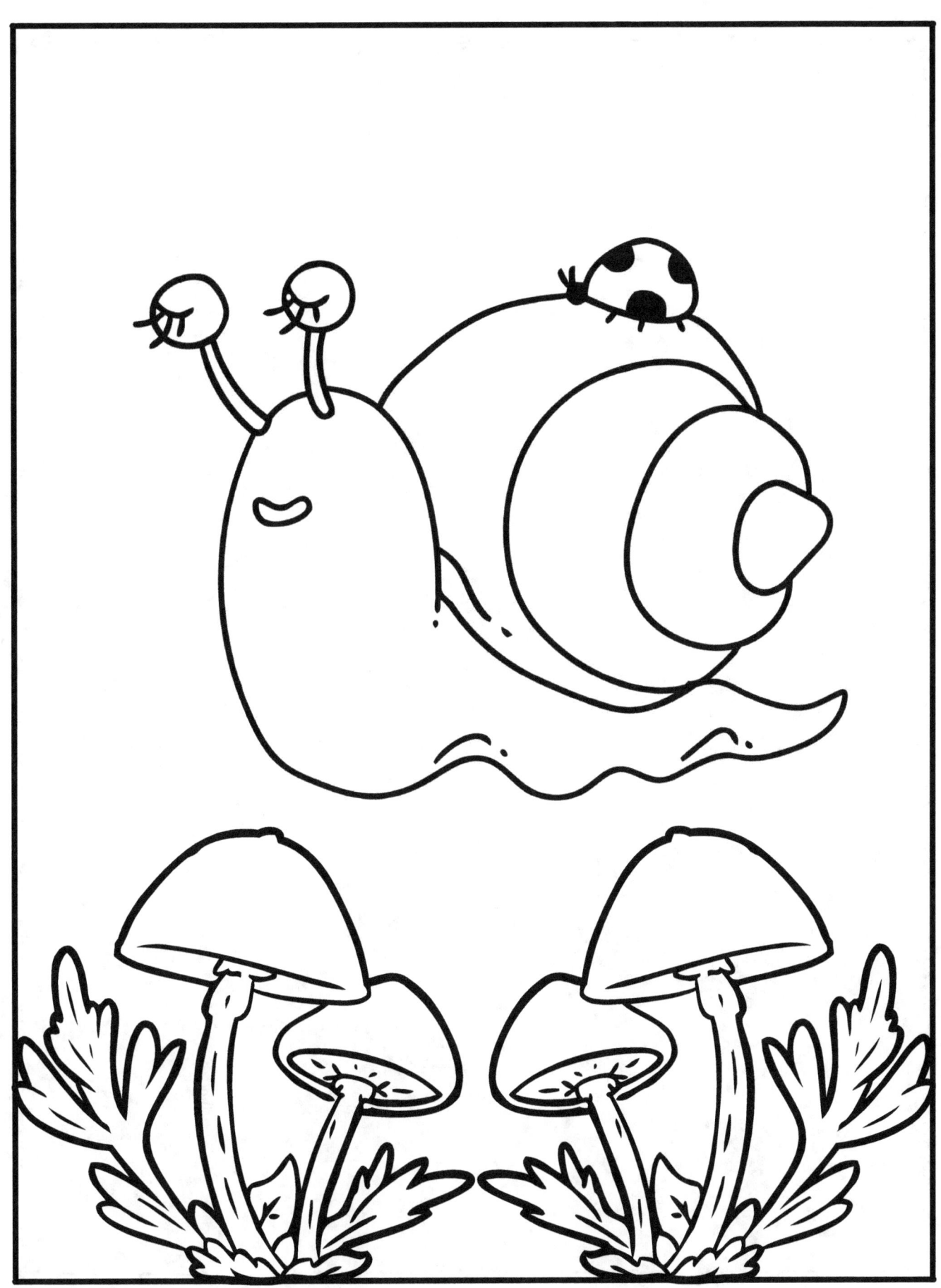

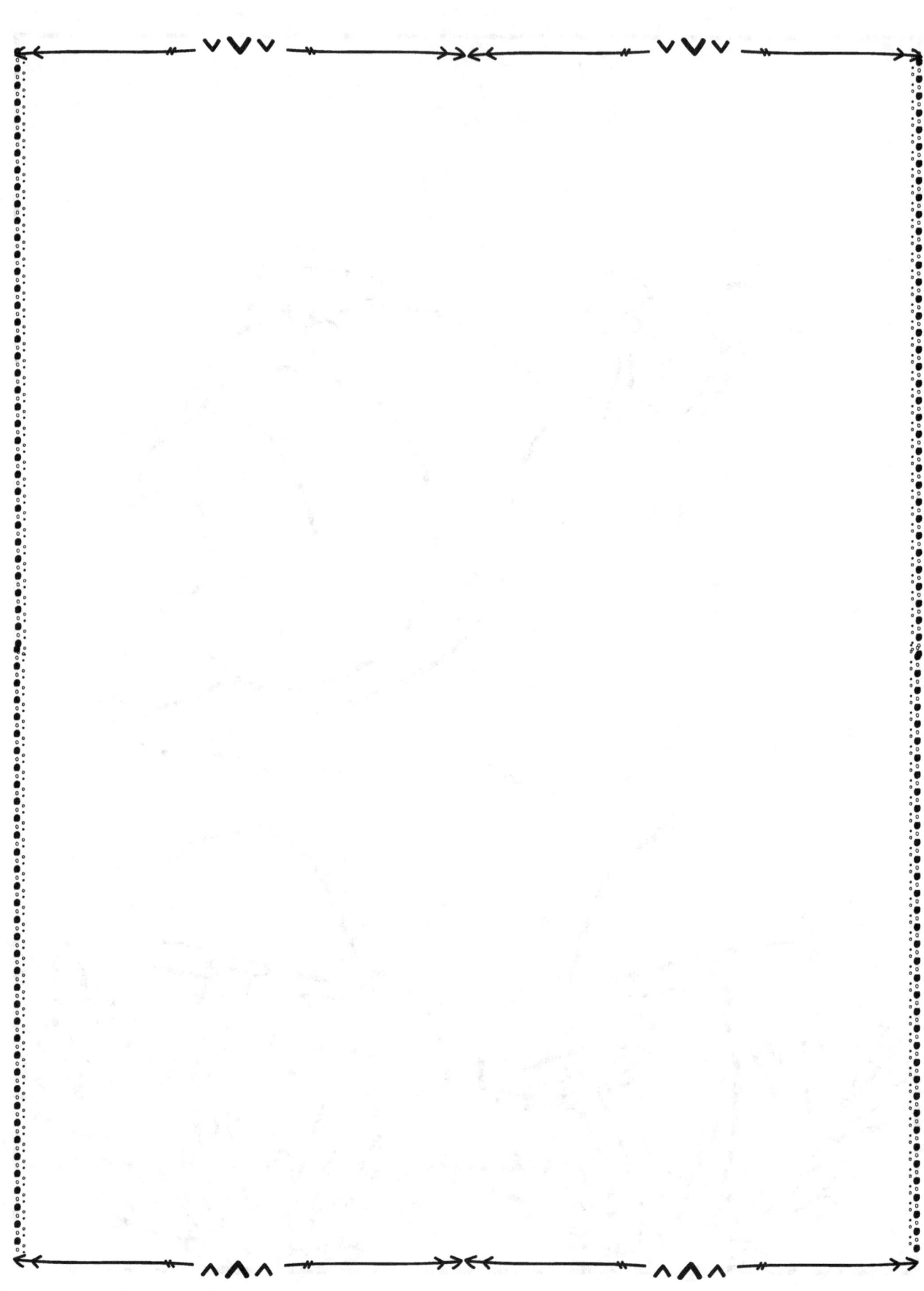

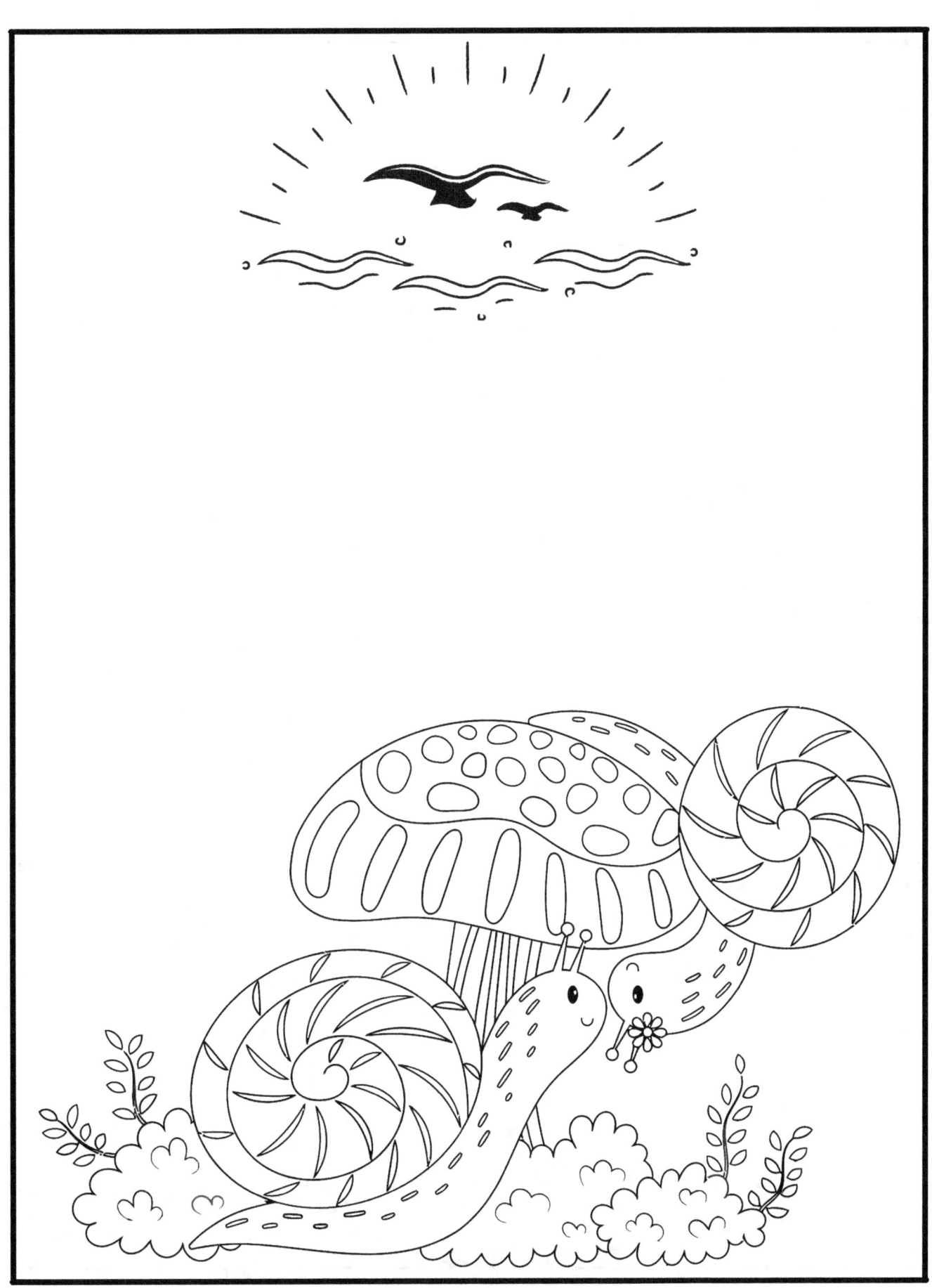

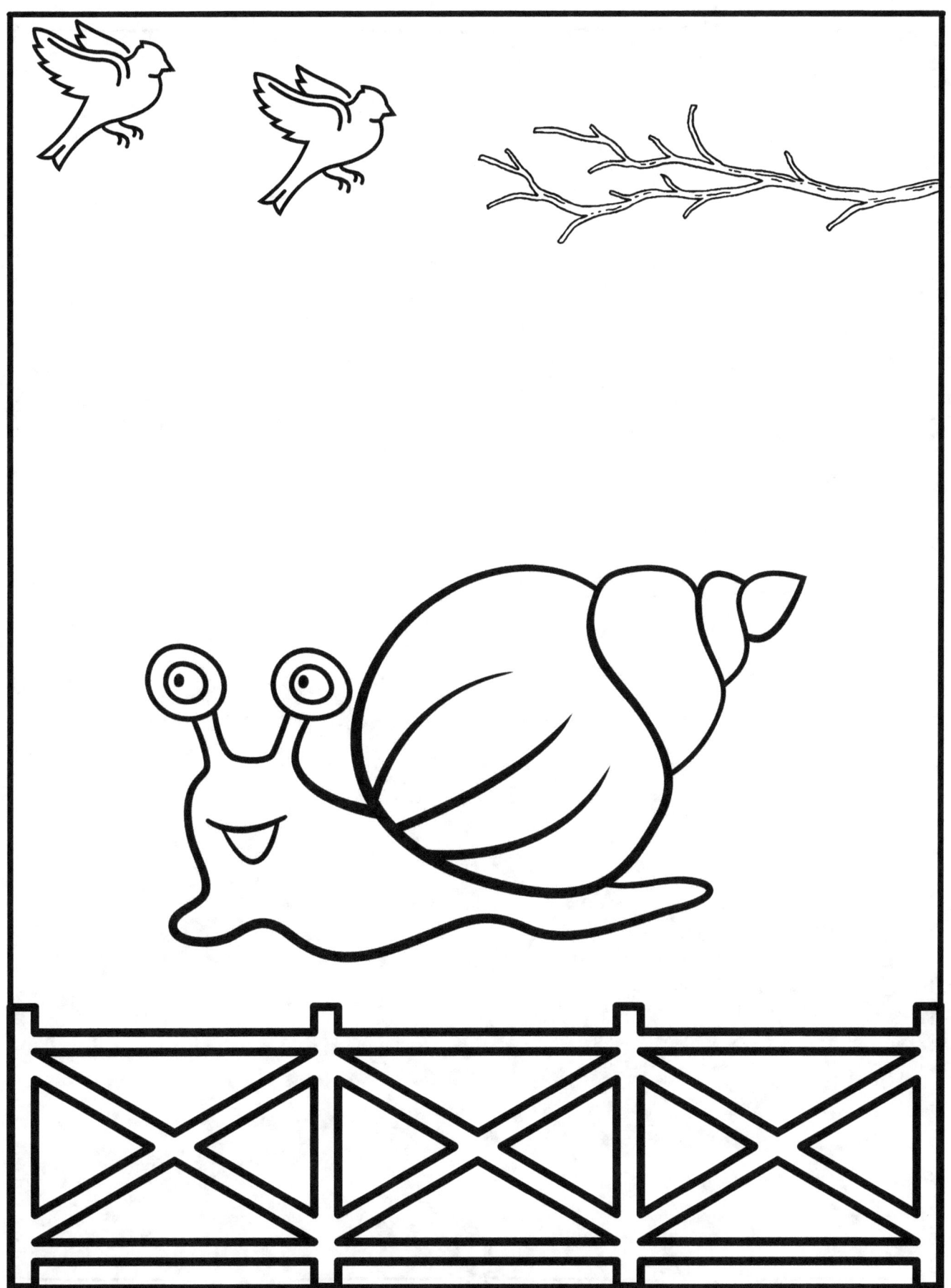

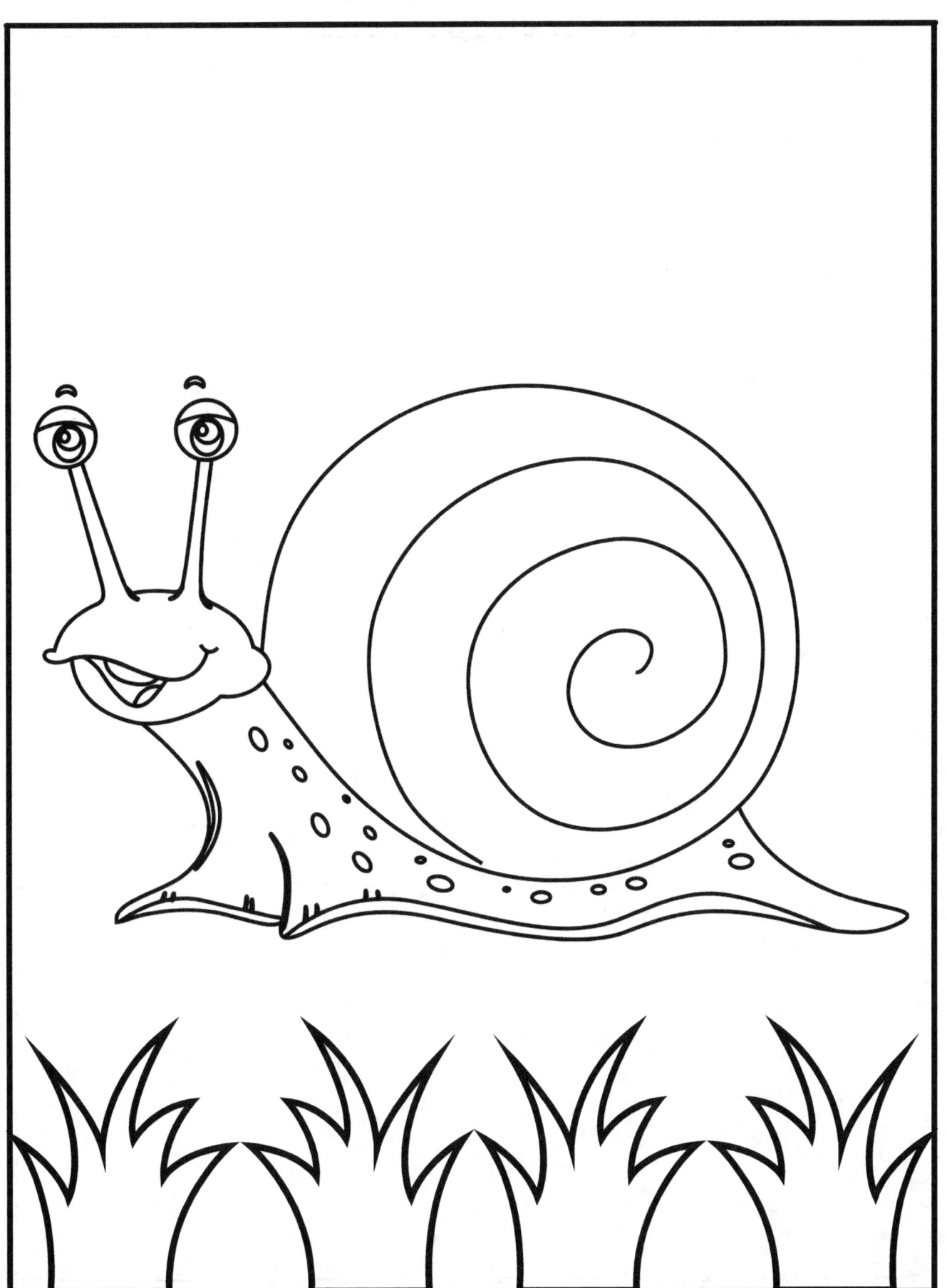

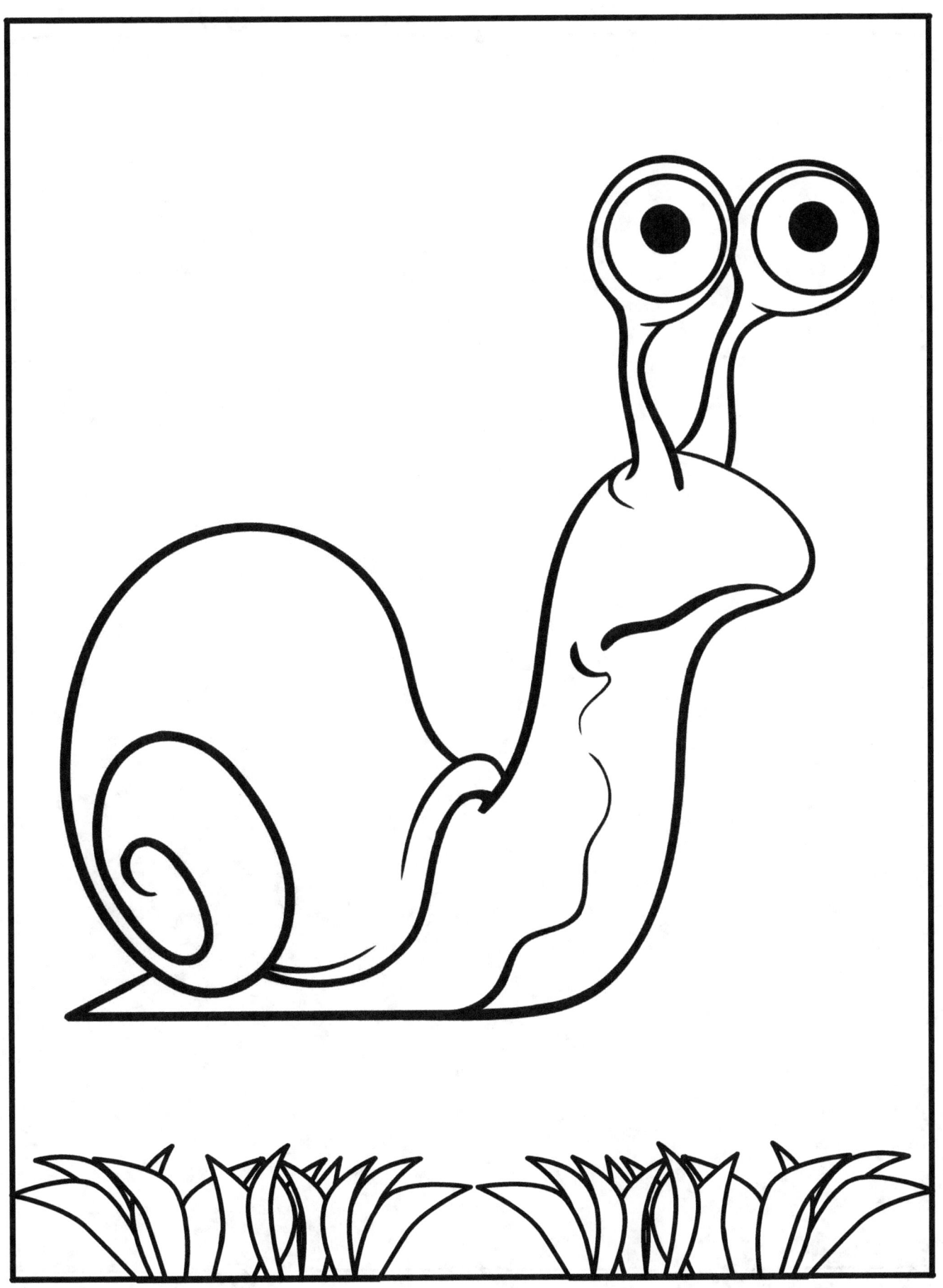

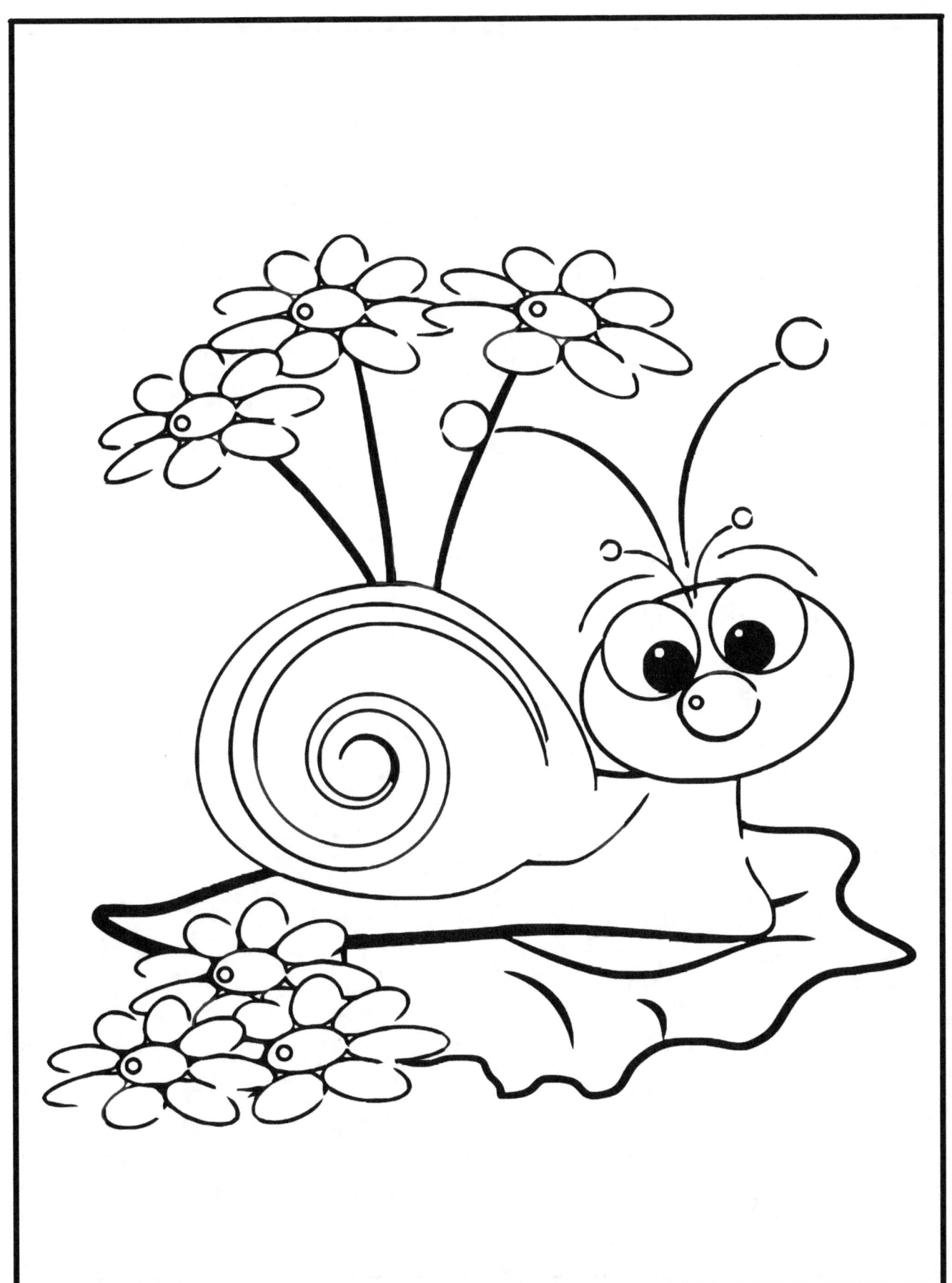

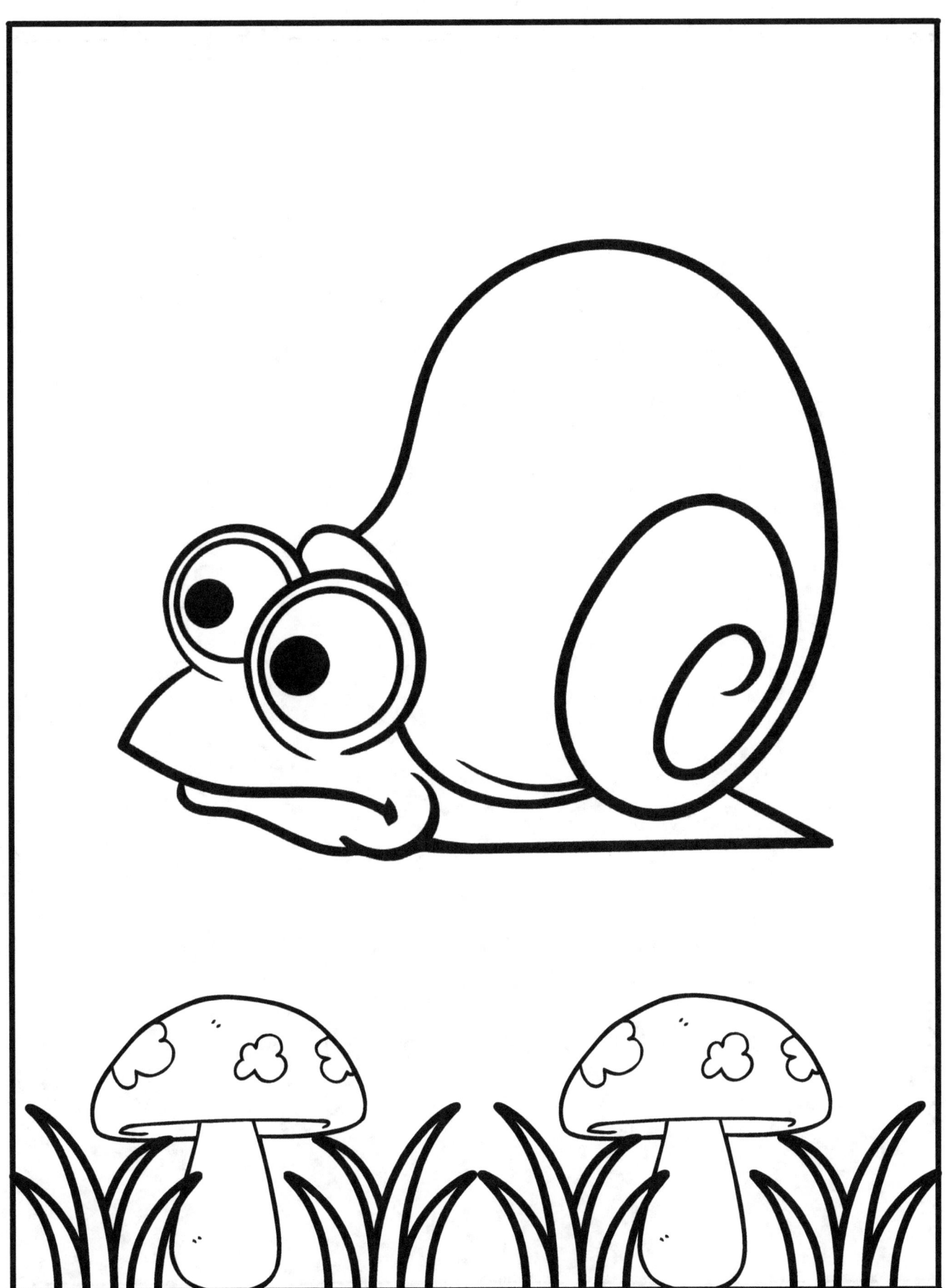

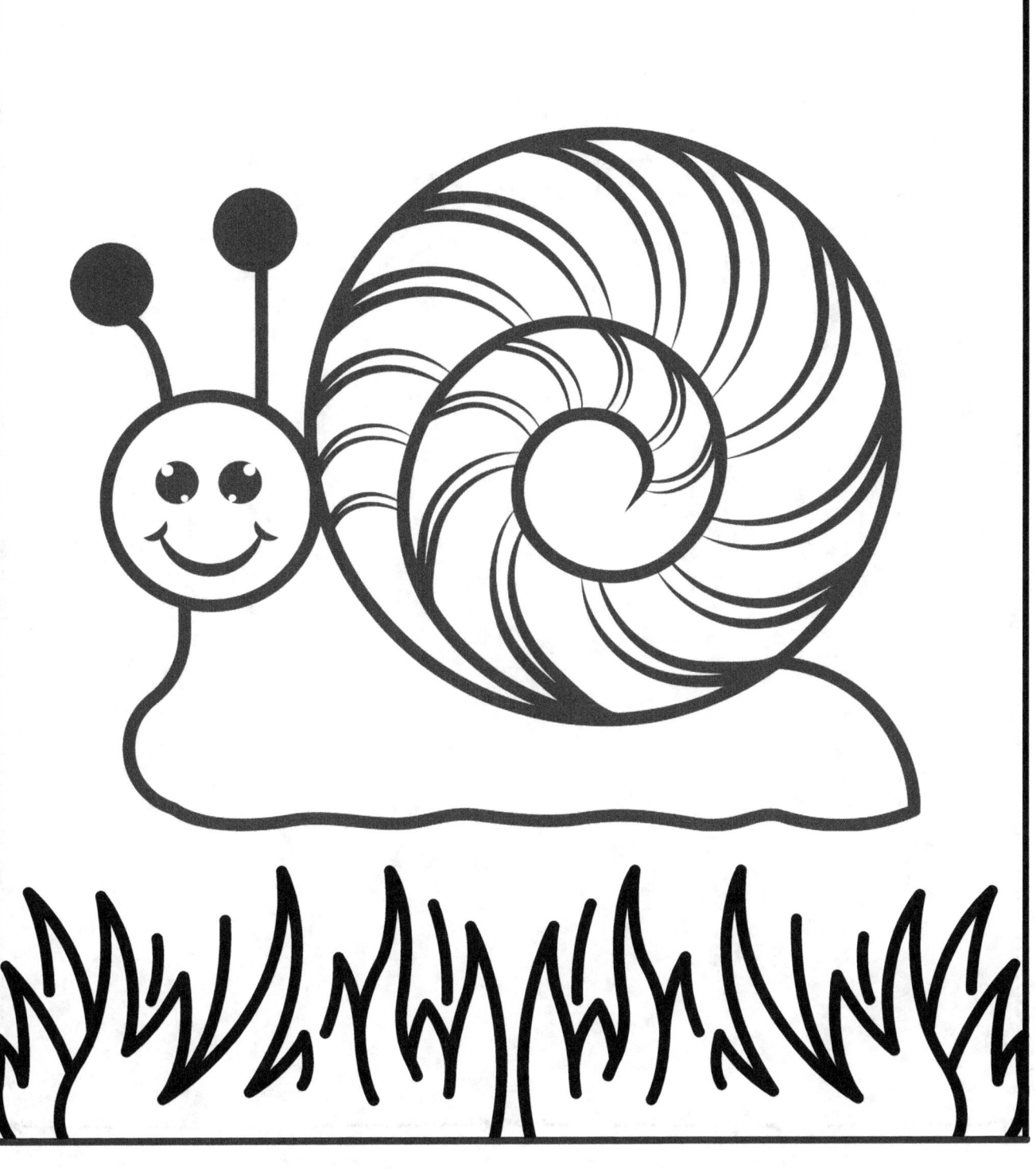

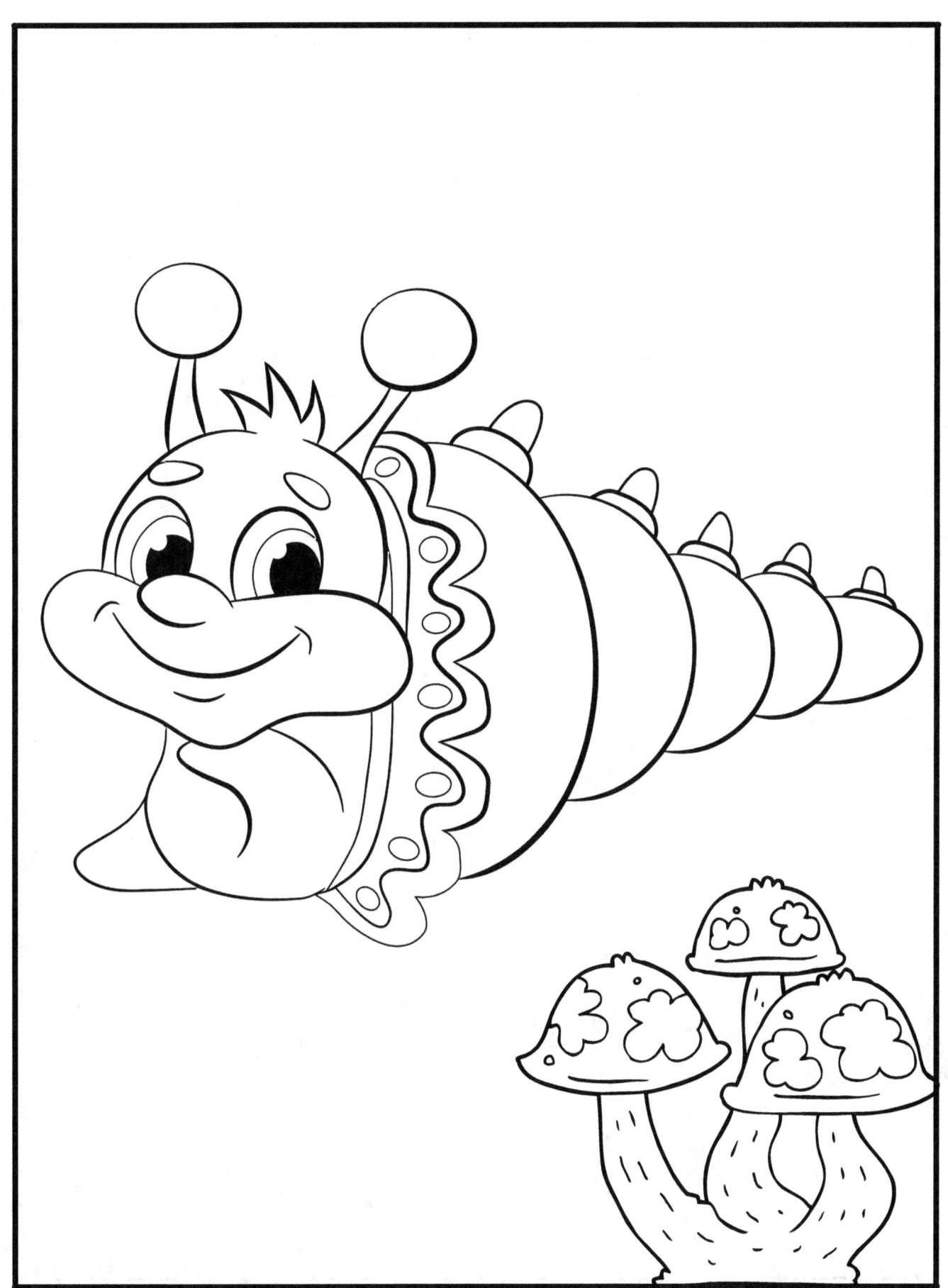

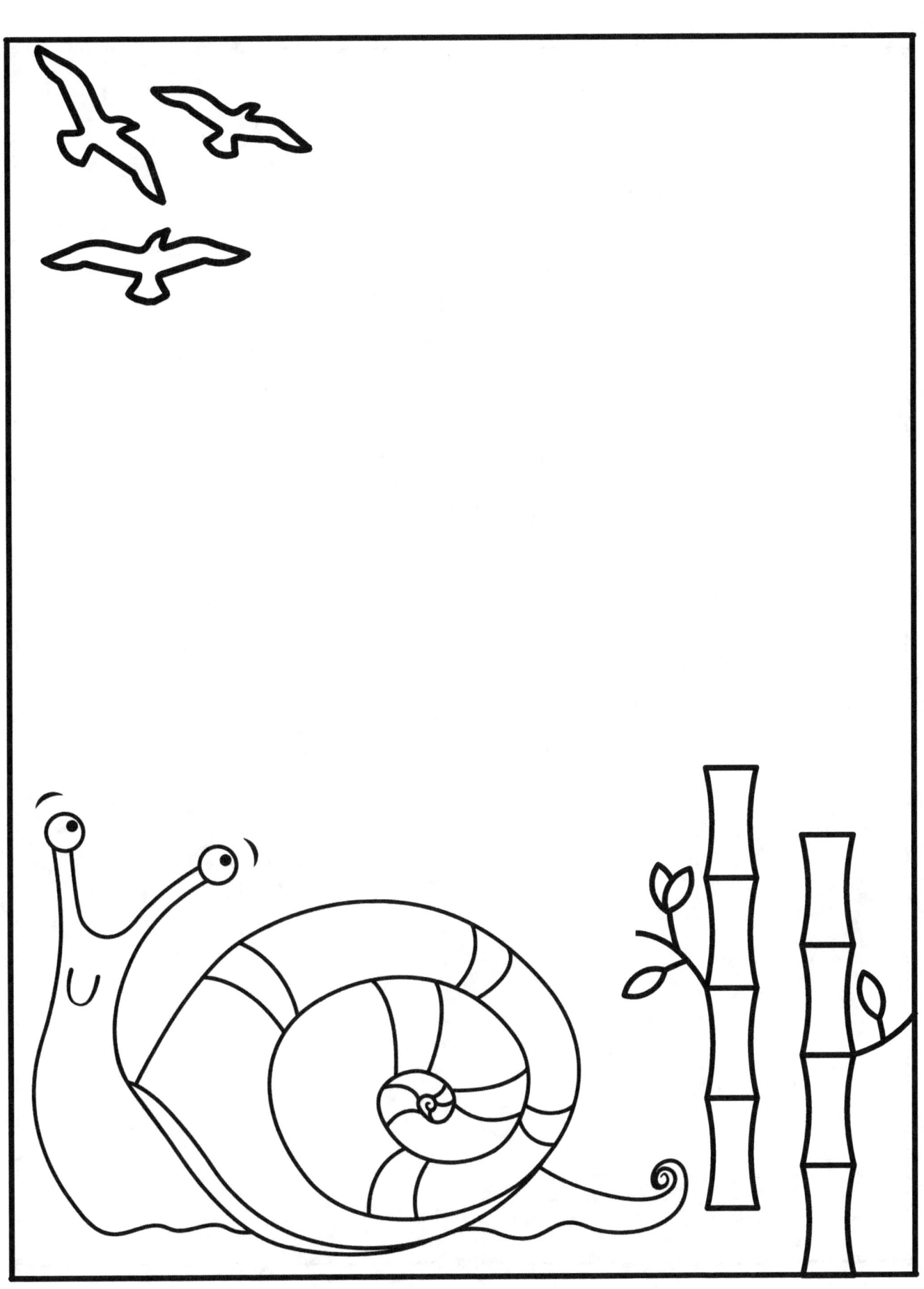

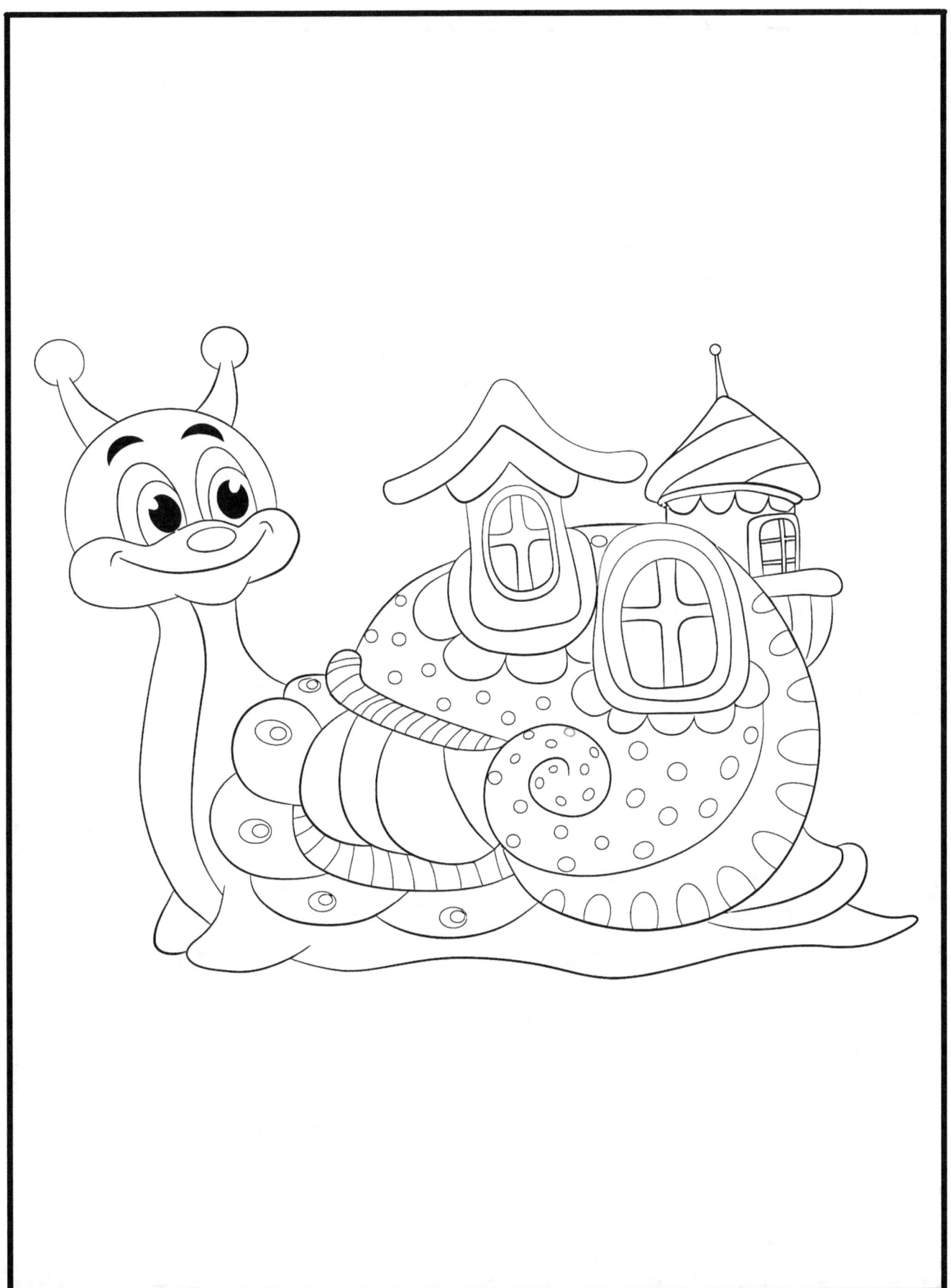

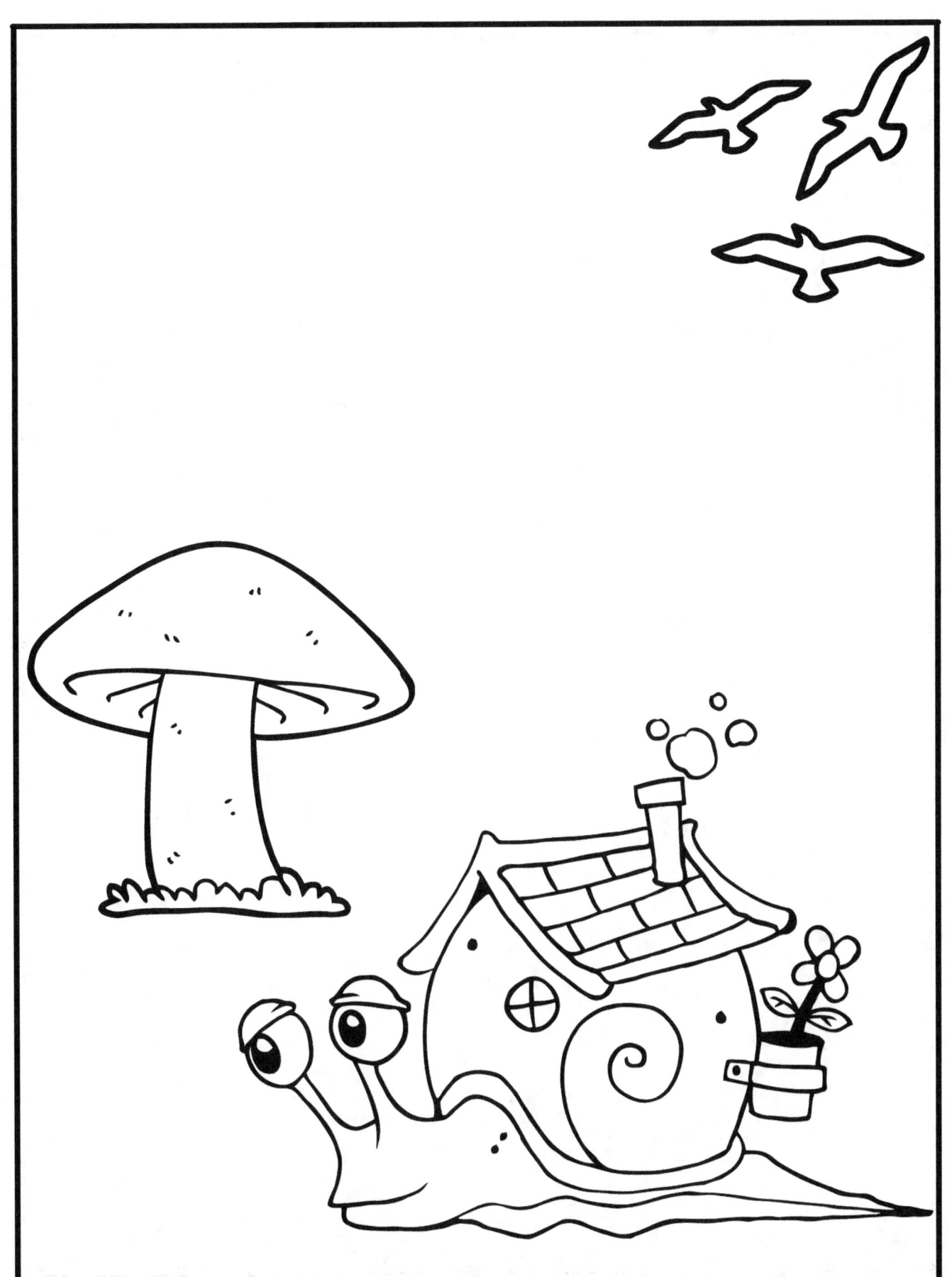

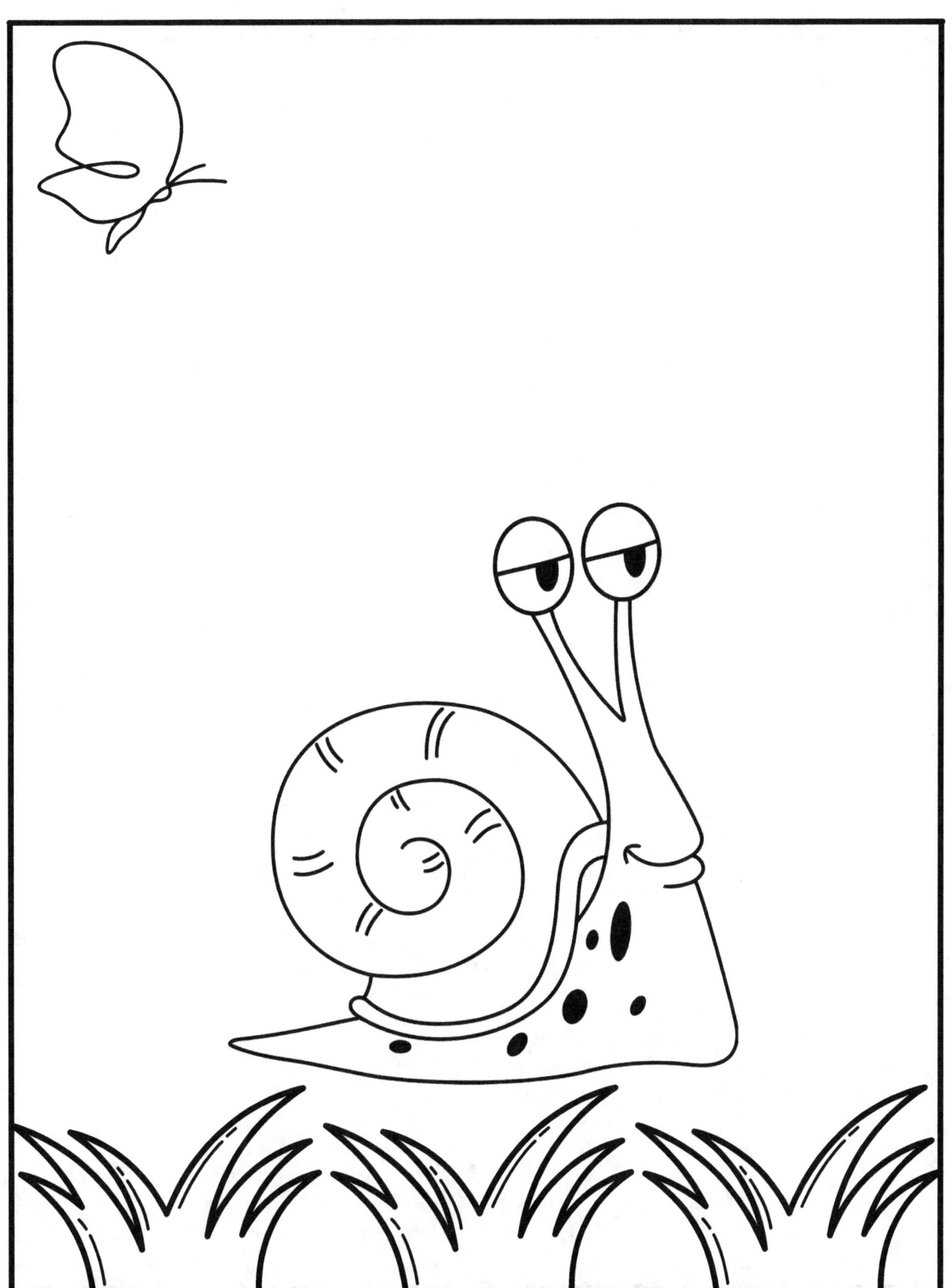

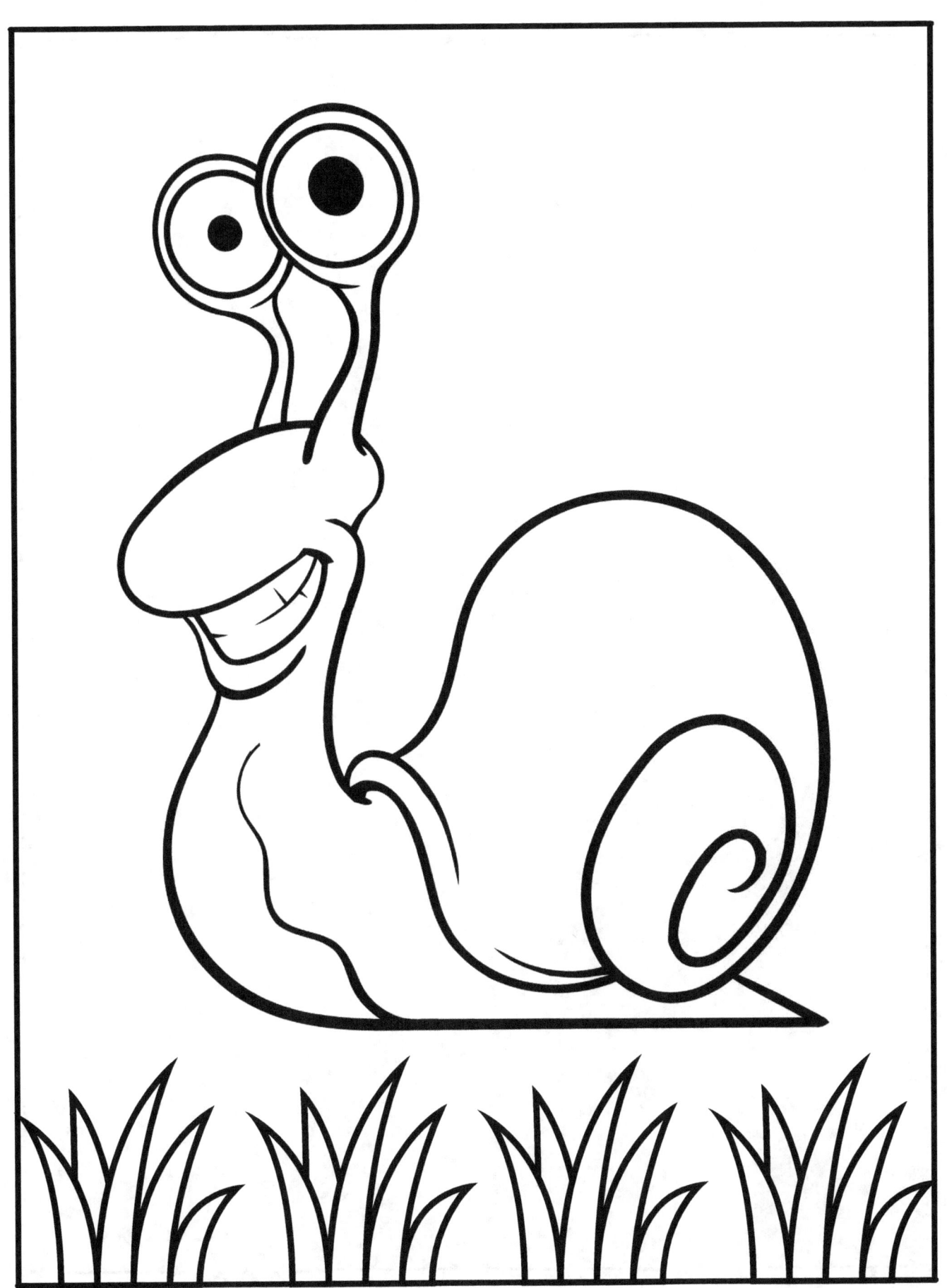

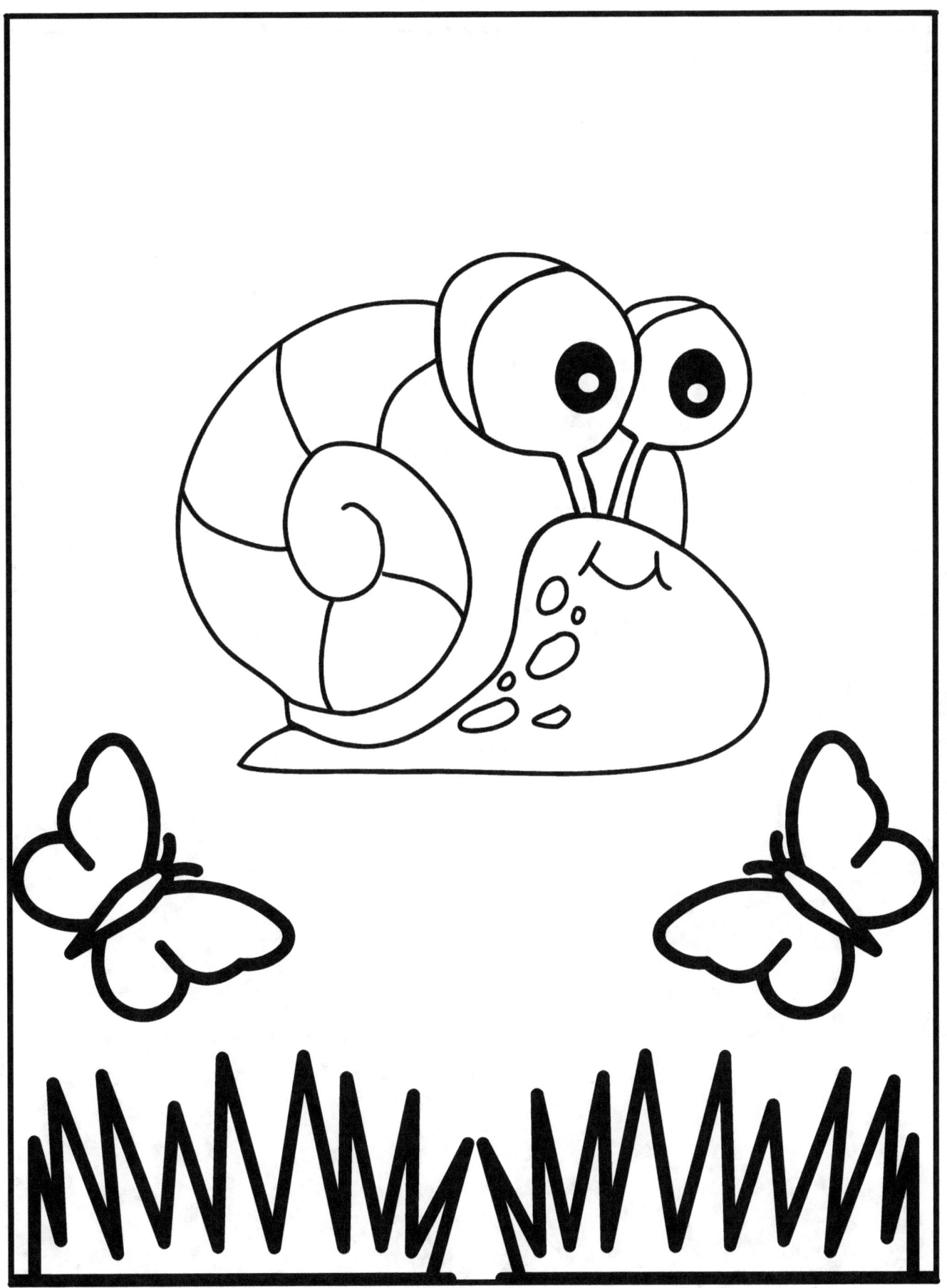

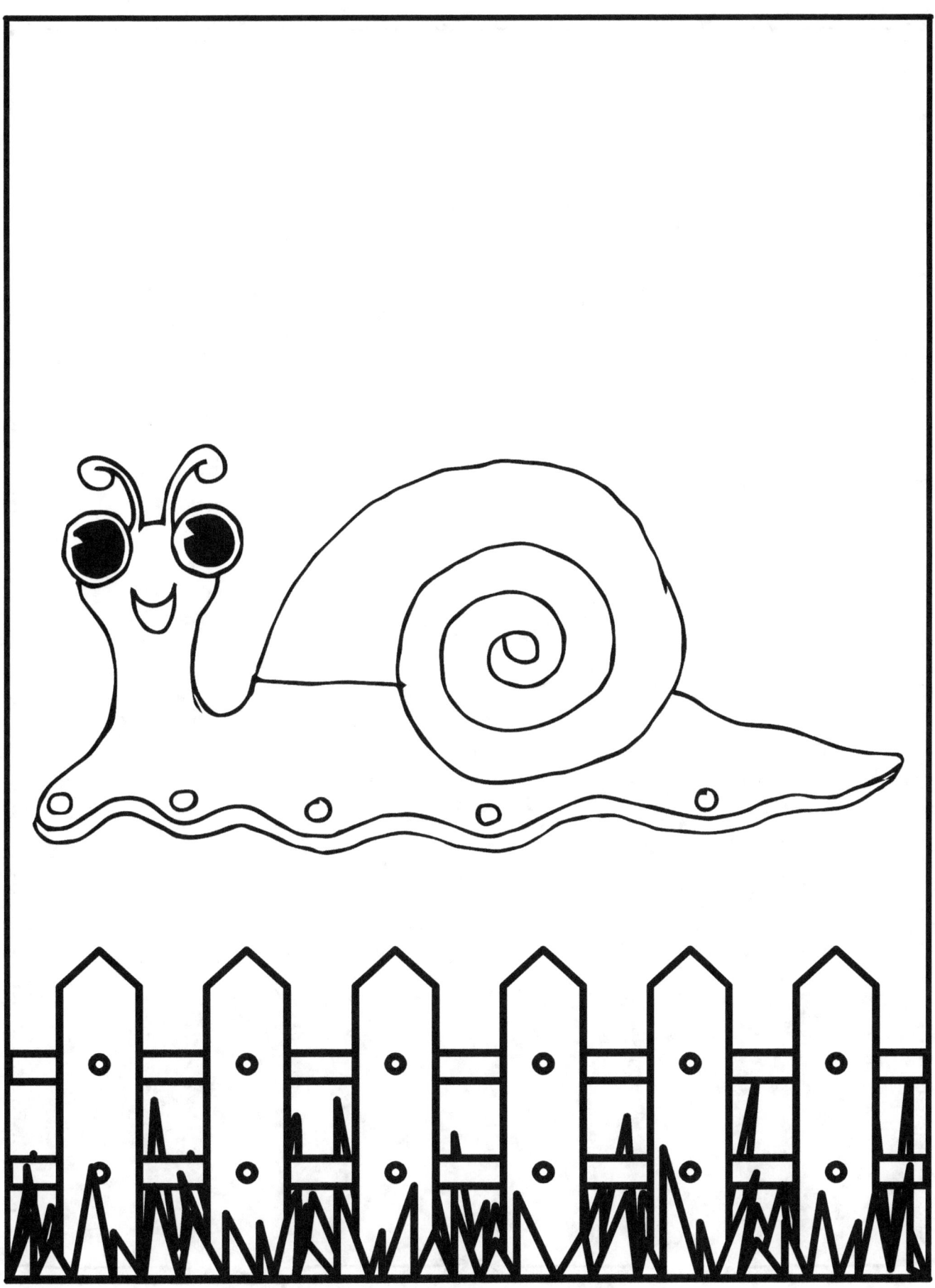

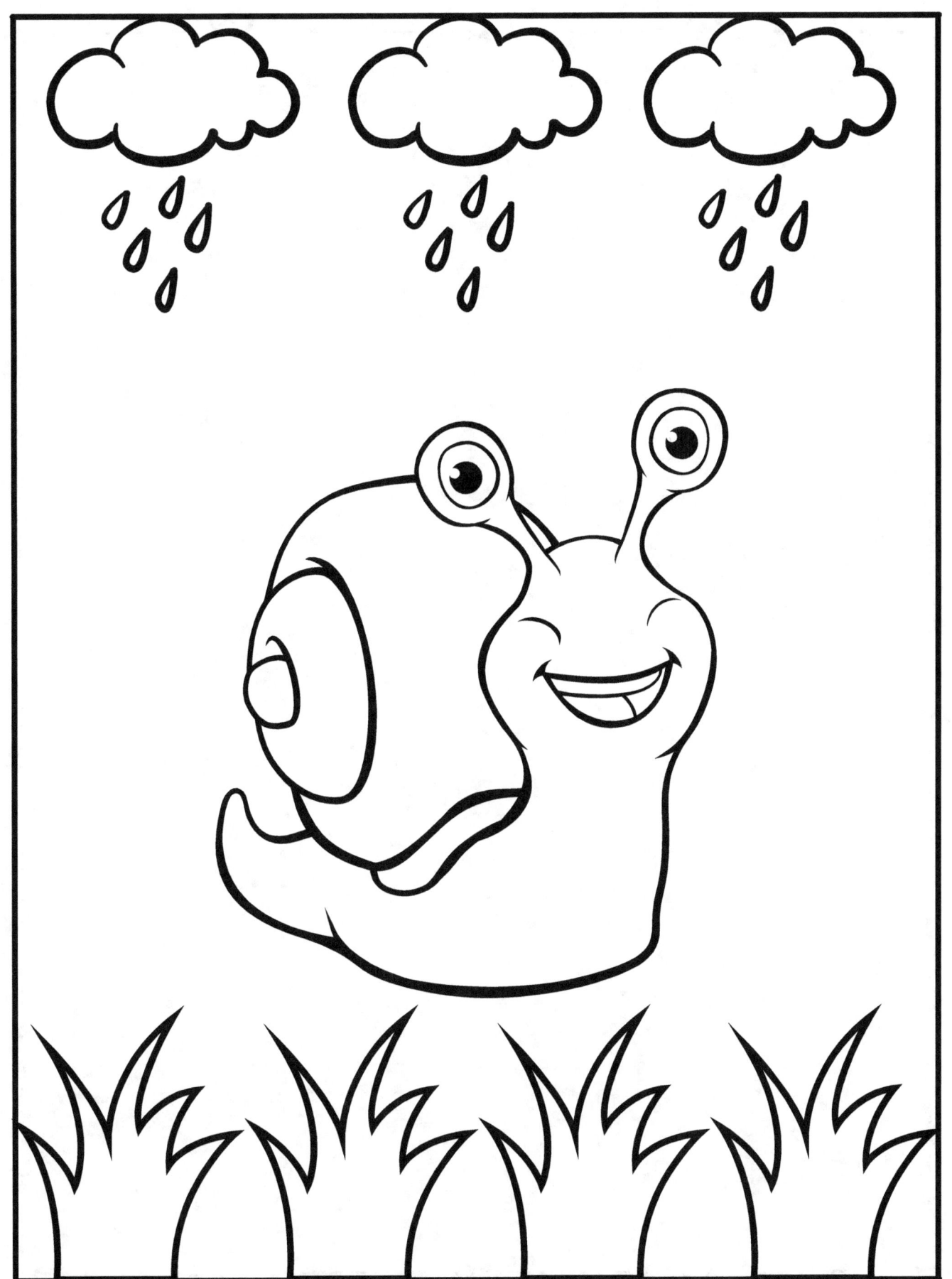

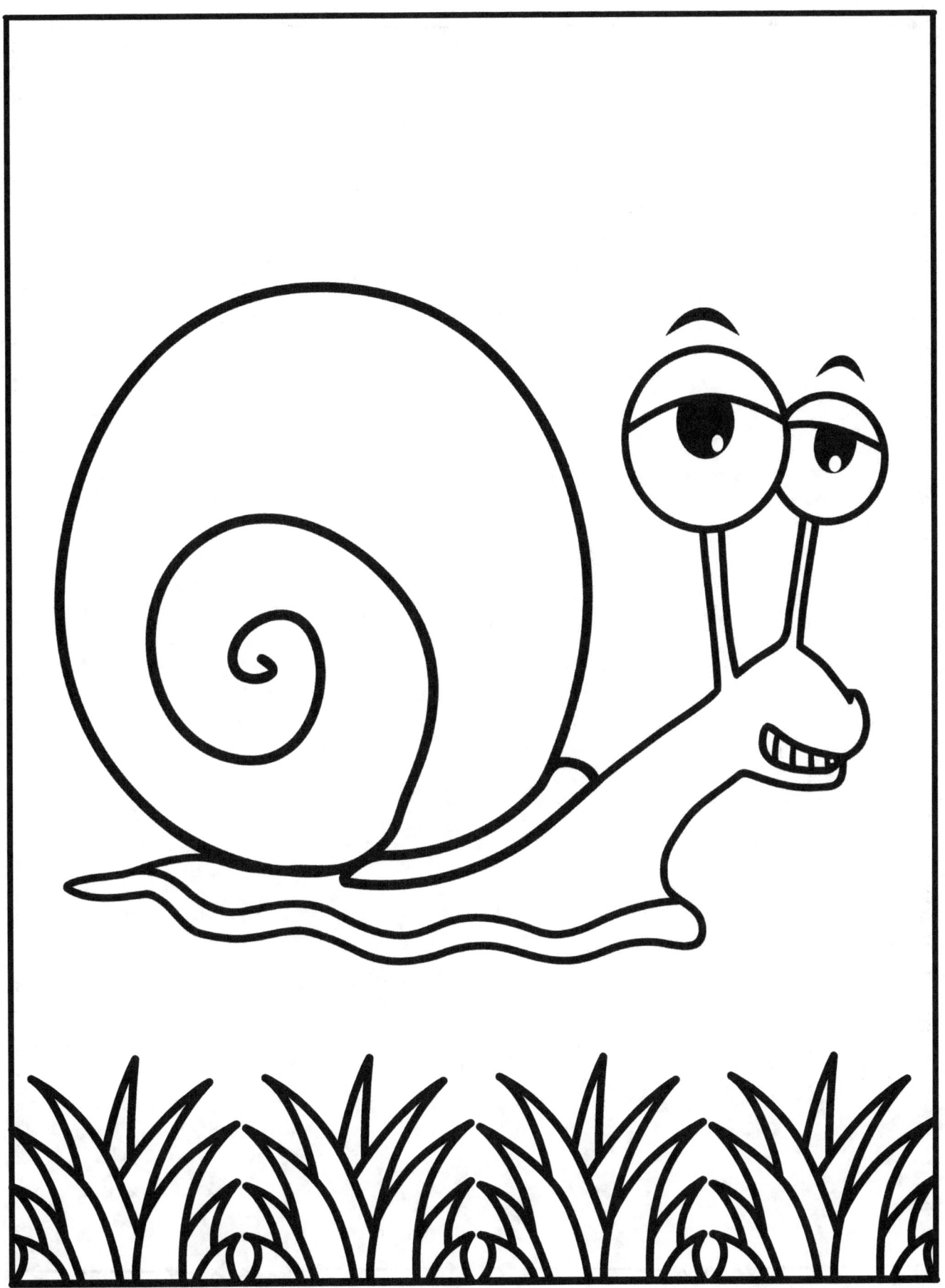

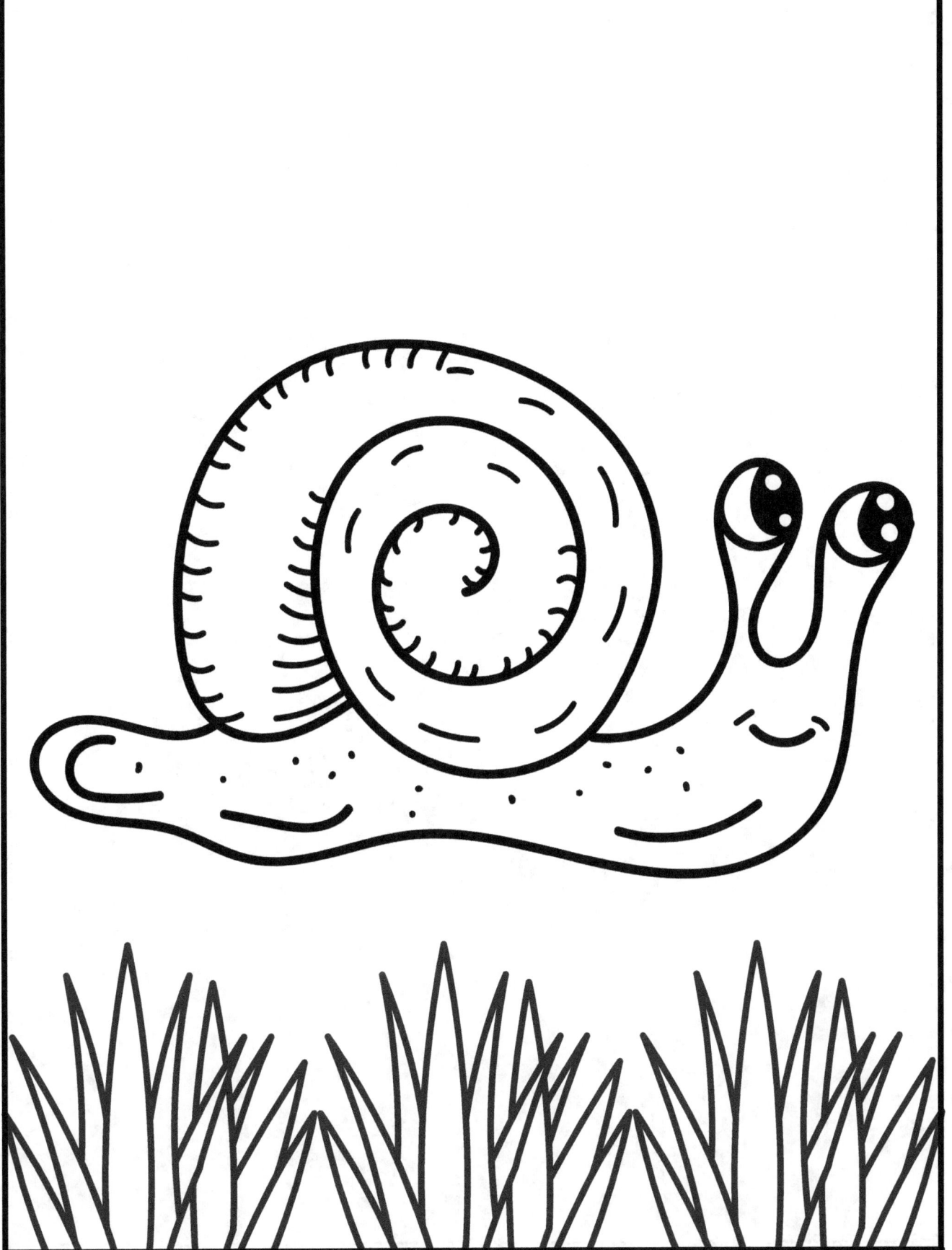

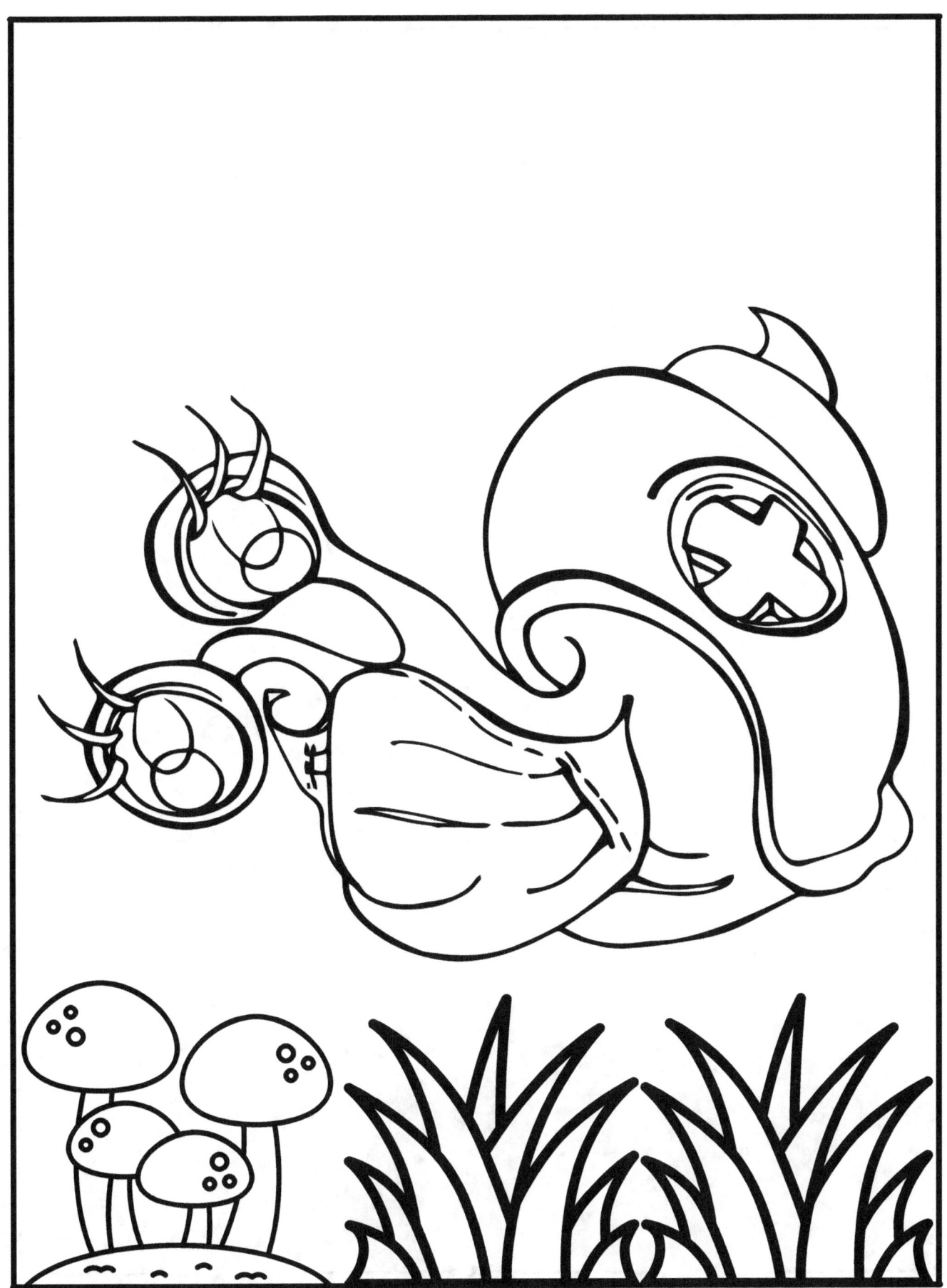

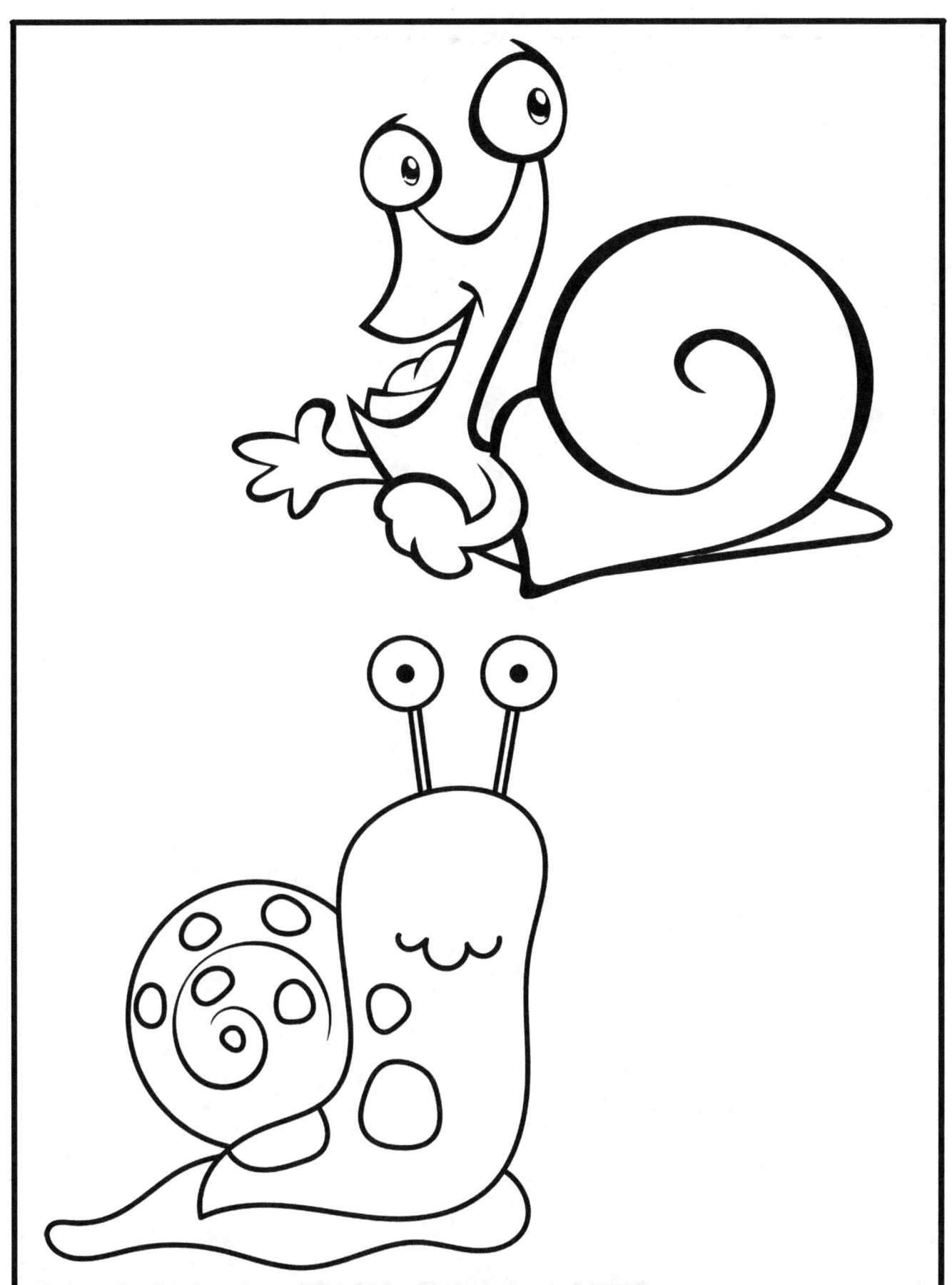

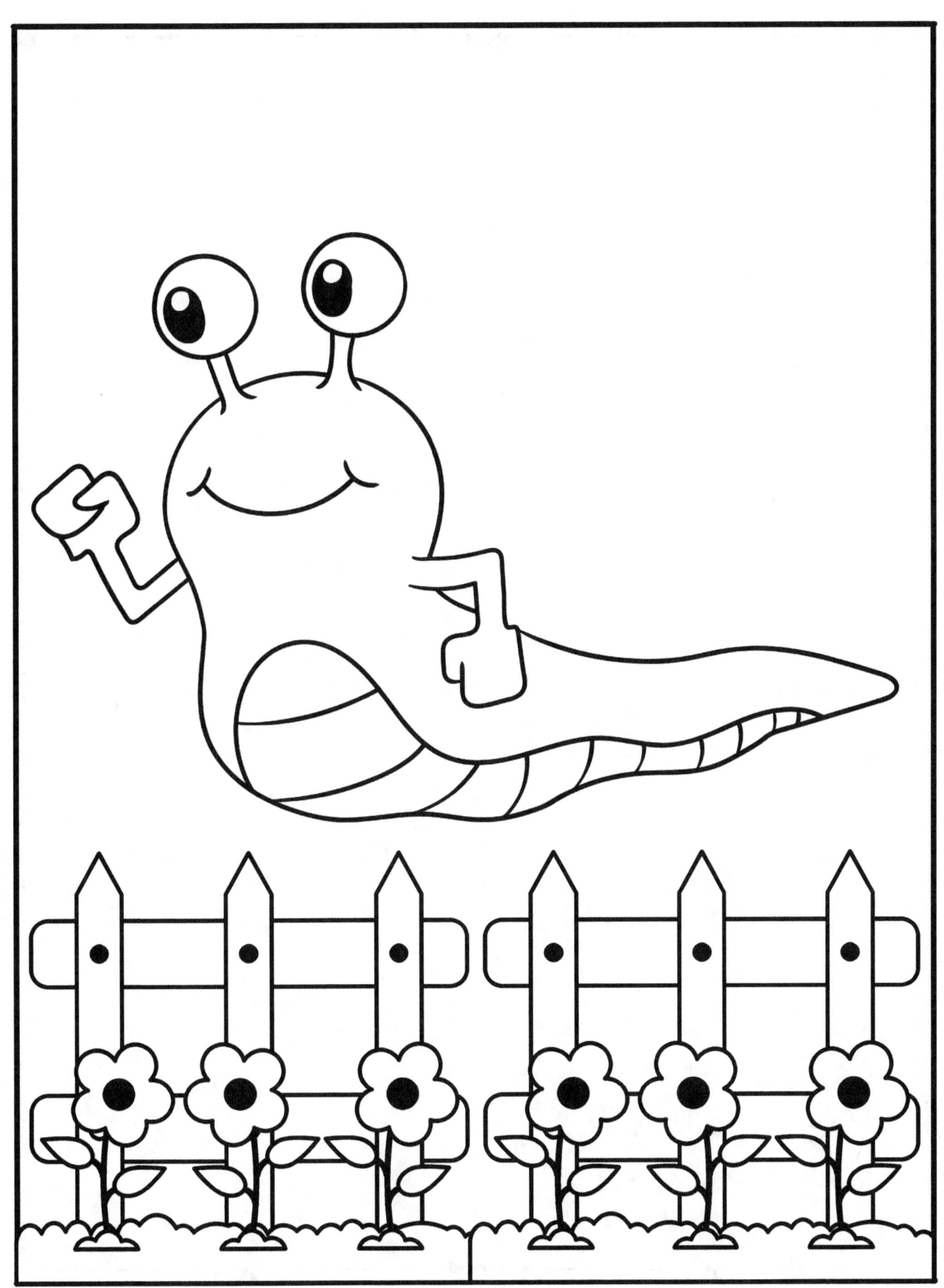

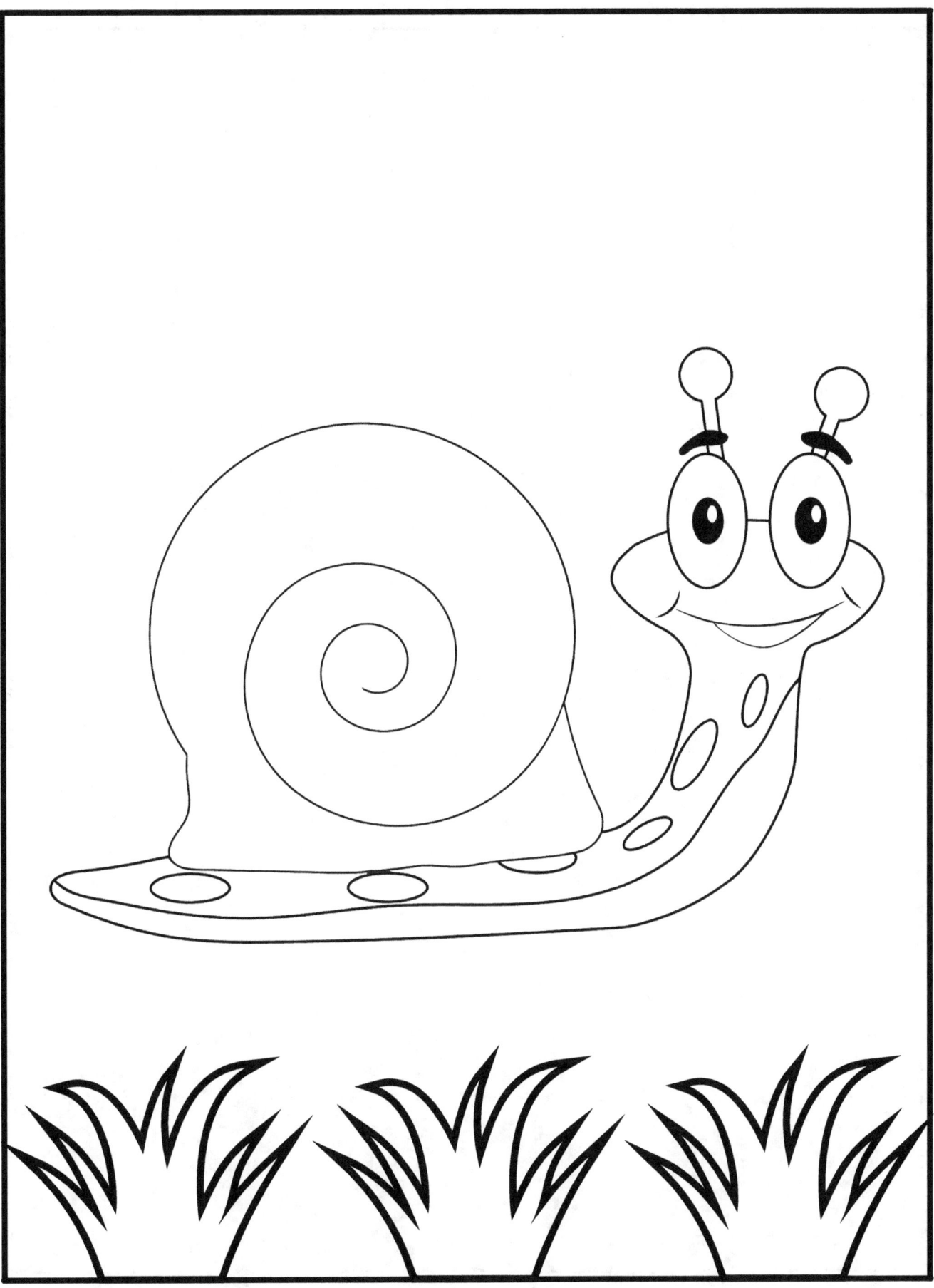

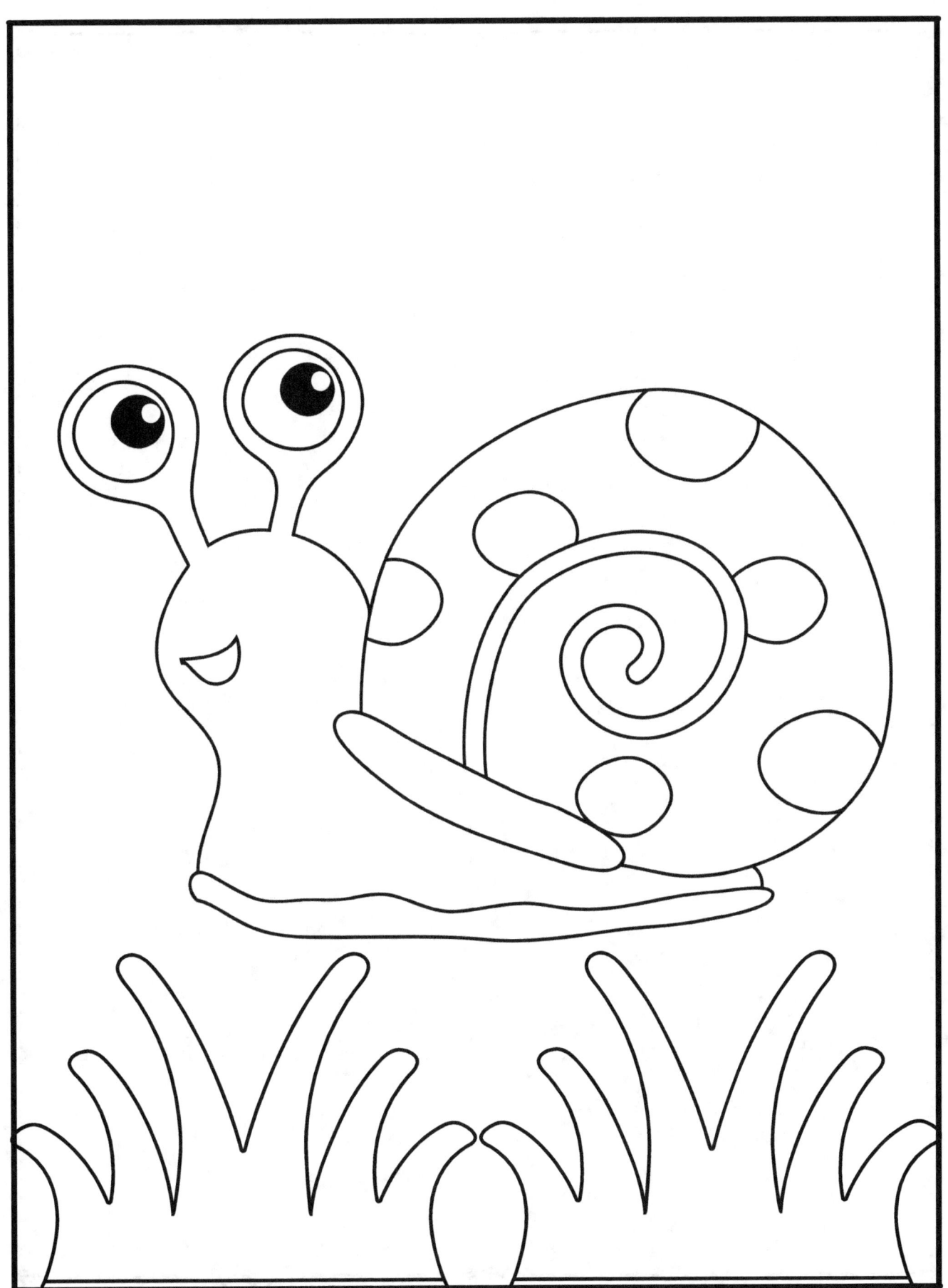

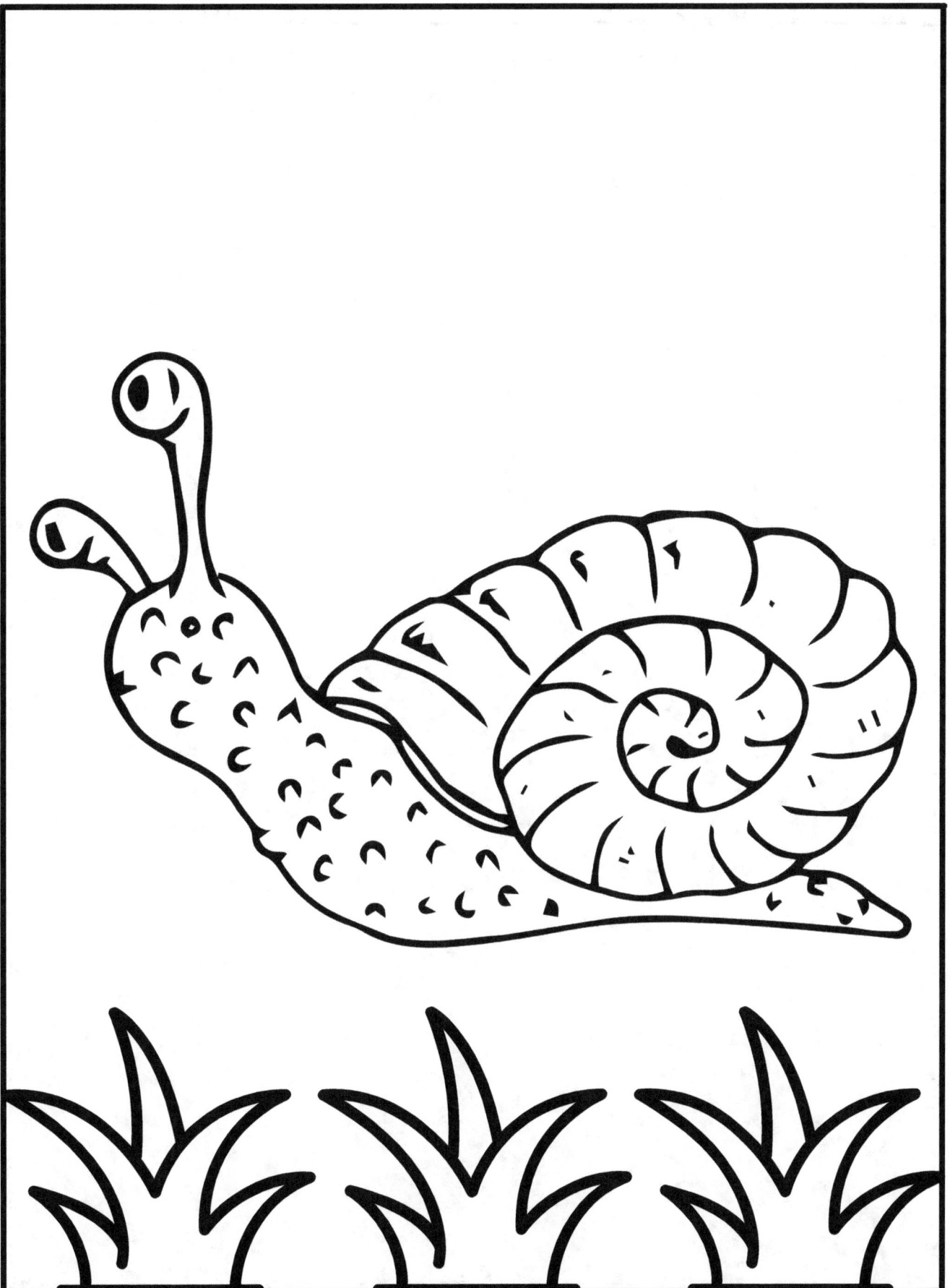

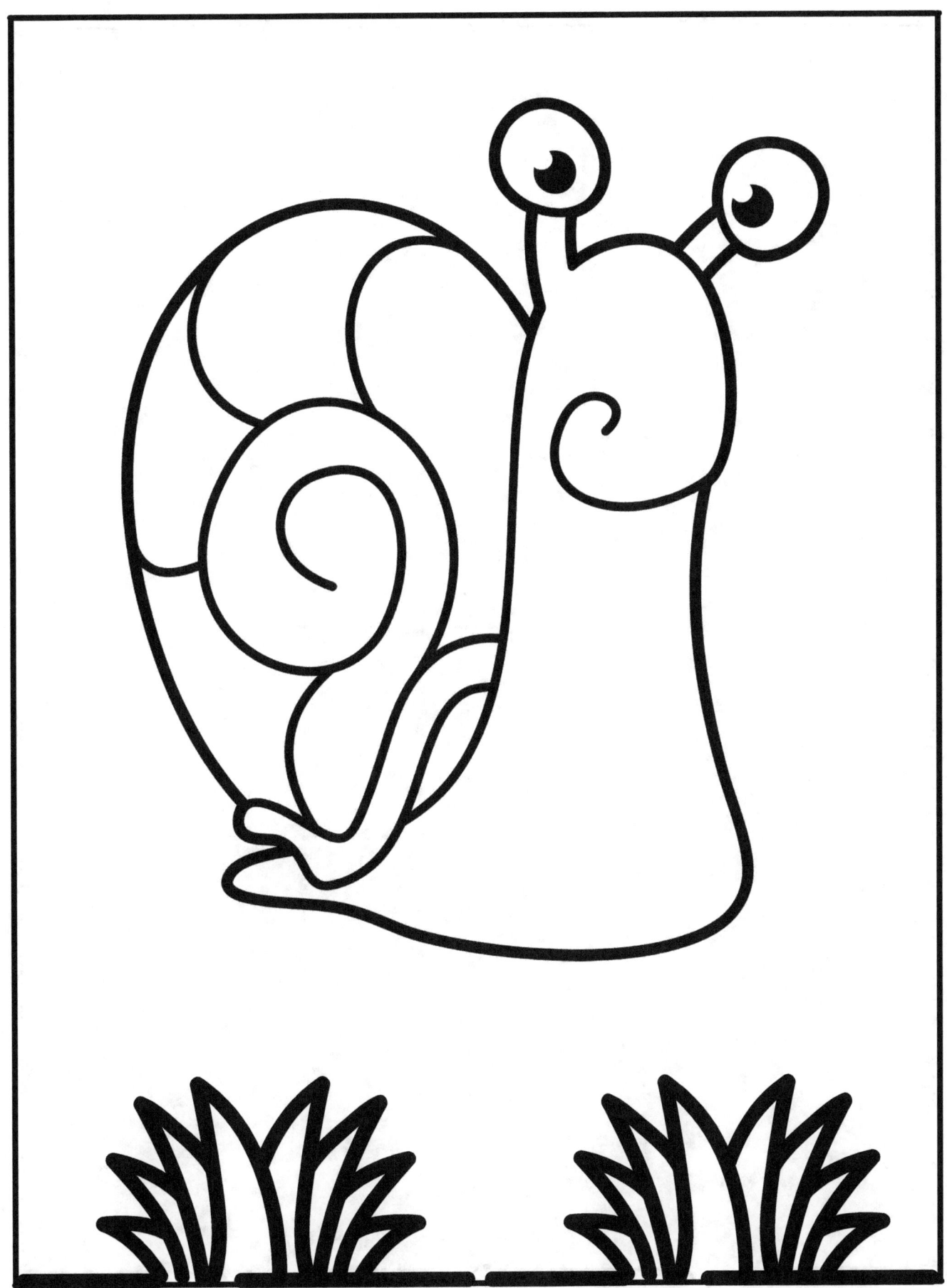

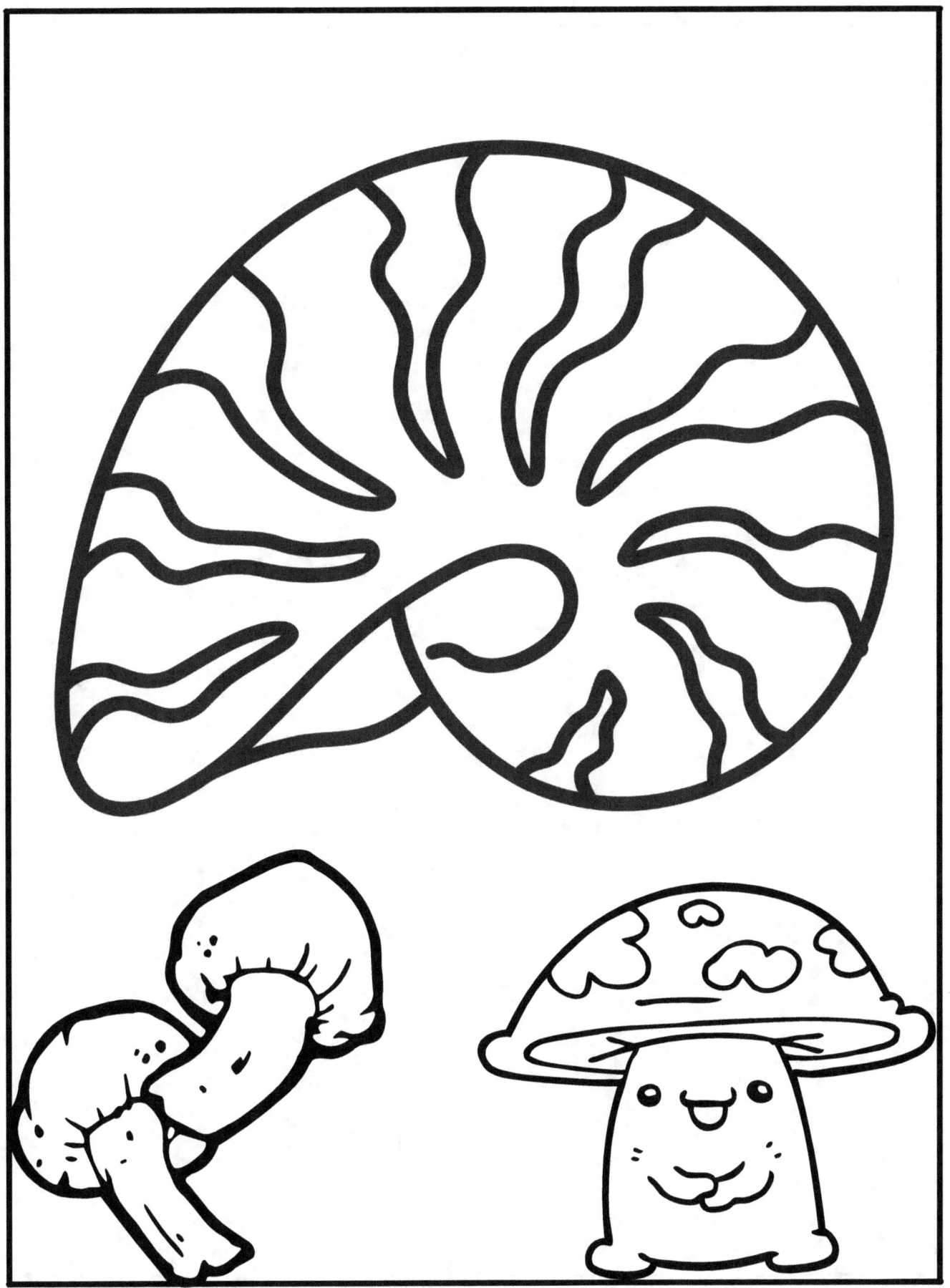

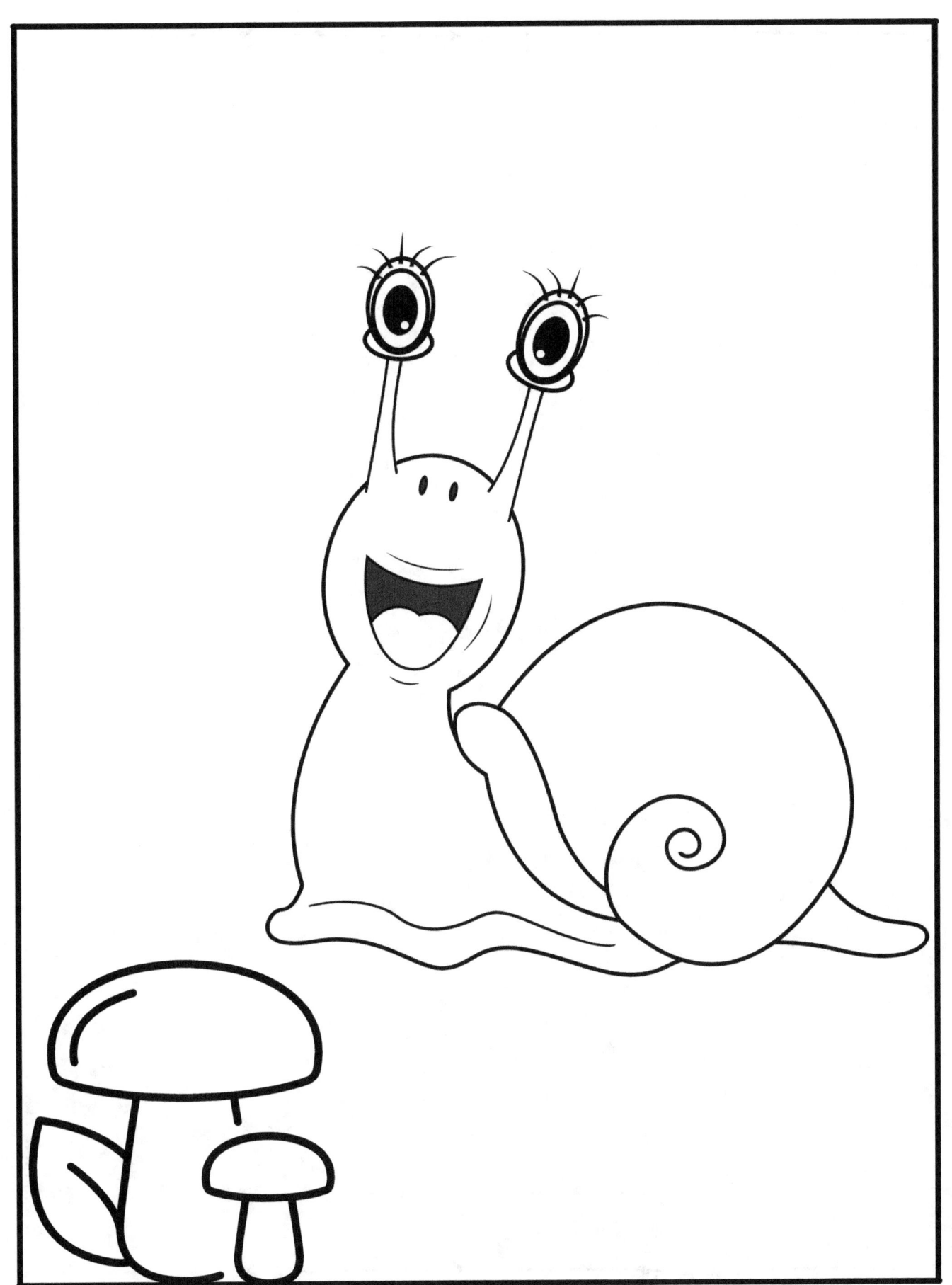

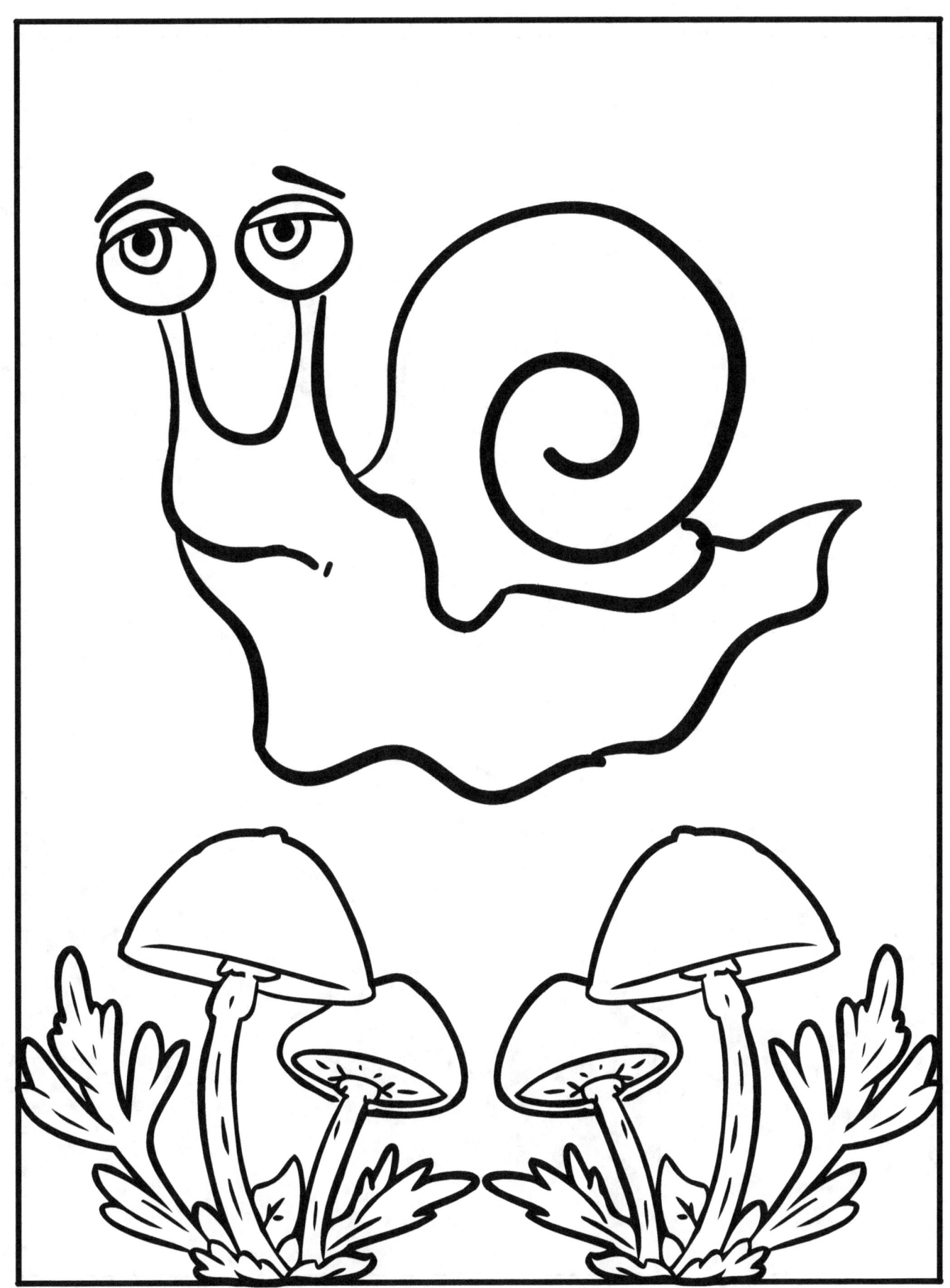

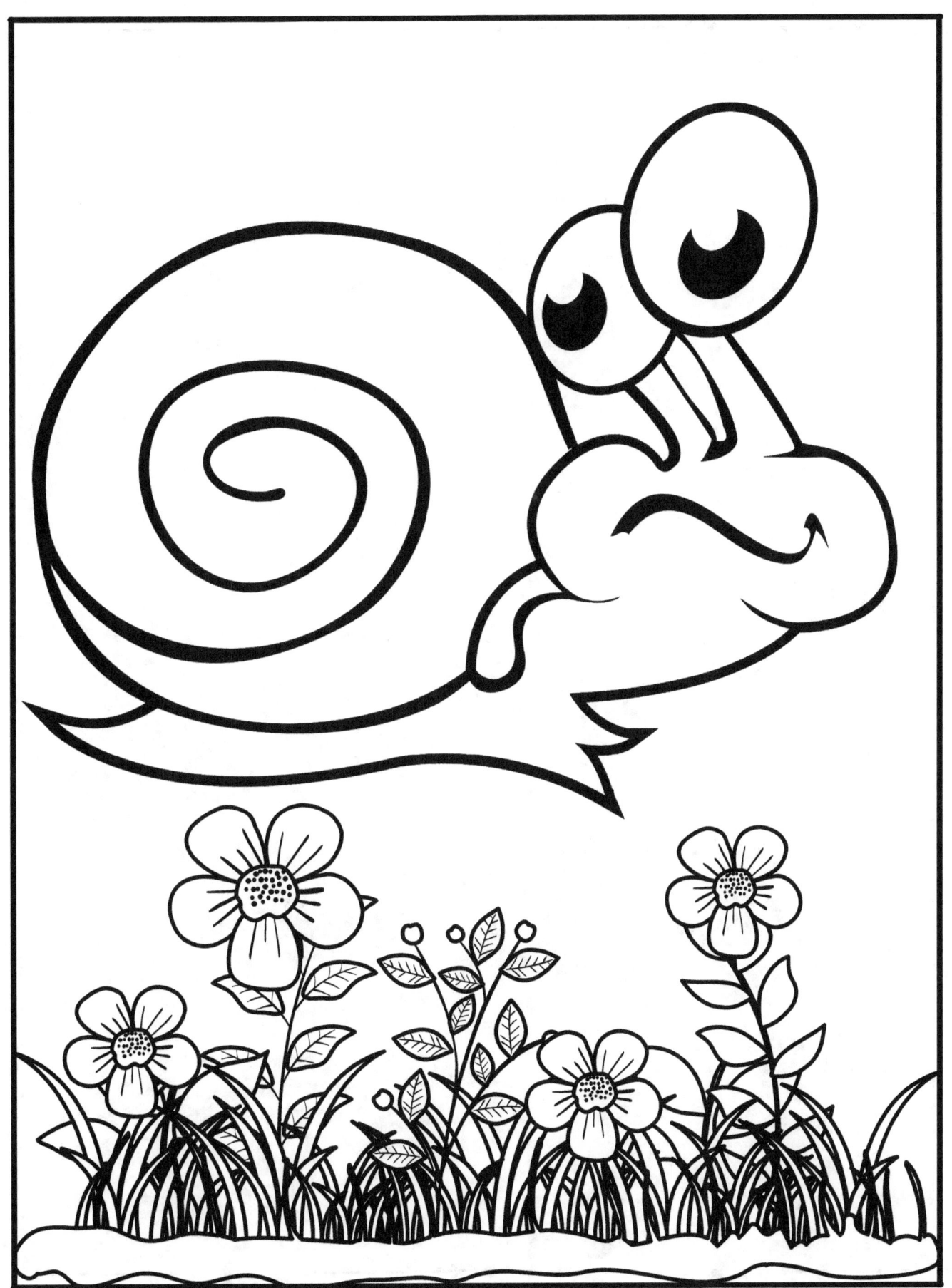

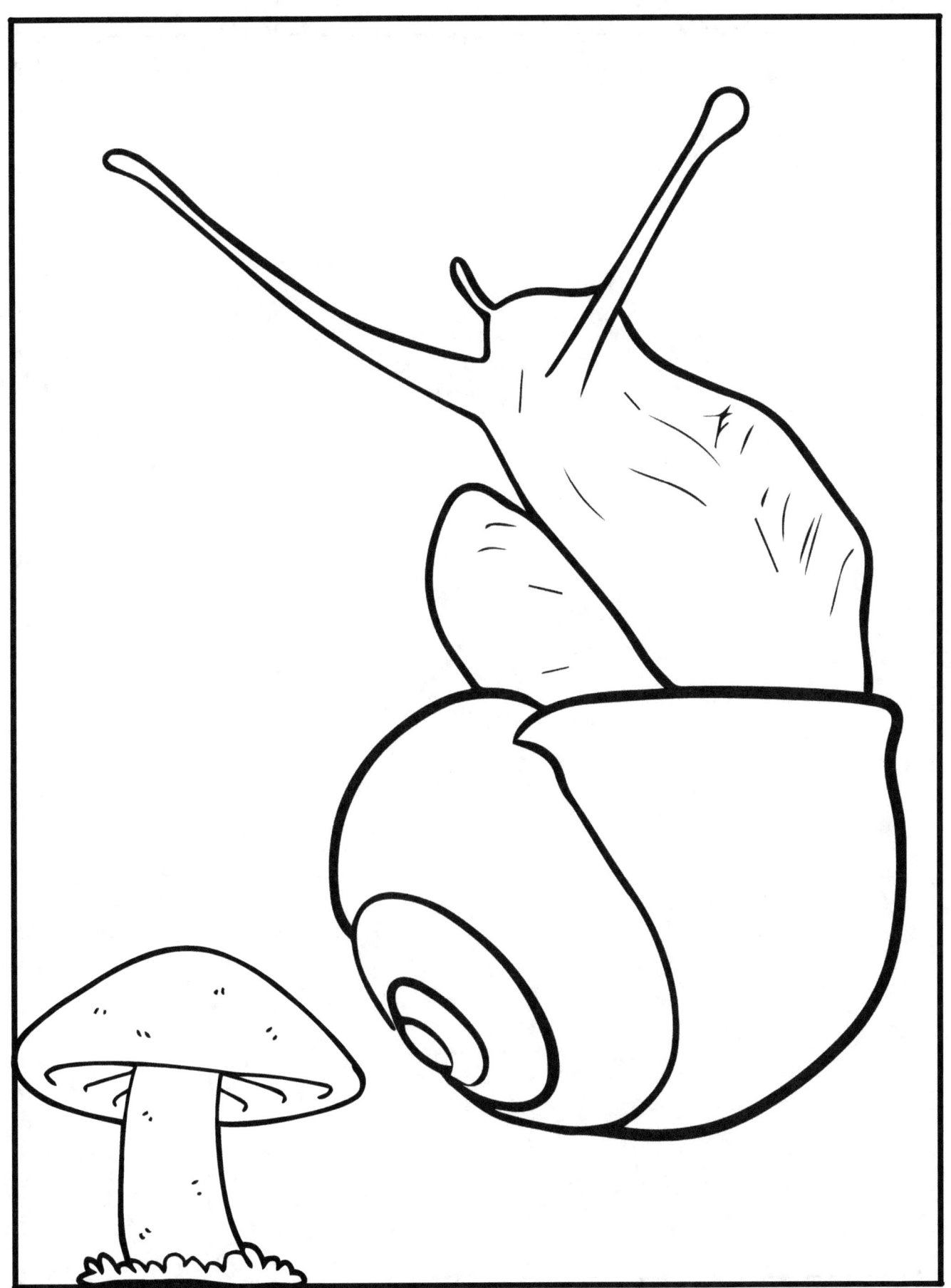

www.ingramcontent.com/pod-product-compliance
Lightning Source LLC
Chambersburg PA
CBHW060437220526
45465CB00008B/3173